THE PLAY SHEET

THE
PLAY SHEET

A Simple Resource for
Overloaded Professionals

BRIAN HURTAK

LIONCREST

PUBLISHING

THE PLAY SHEET

A Simple Resource for Overloaded Professionals
First Edition

ISBN   978-1-5445-4681-0   *Hardcover*
       978-1-5445-4680-3   *Paperback*
       978-1-5445-4682-7   *Ebook*

CONTENTS

PREGAME

On "any given Sunday" (okay, more like a regular Sunday afternoon a few years ago), something ordinary that I had seen thousands of times before ended up completely changing my approach to professional development.

I was sitting on my couch, a football game on the TV, my laptop in front of me, buried in printouts as I prepped for the work week ahead. It was comical, looking at my calendar and its dizzying mix of colors from my attempt to color-code my schedule by priority. I was double-booked here, had a conflict there, and of course had back-to-back meetings that did not allow any prep time between one big engagement and the next. I saw that I had several scheduled interviews for critical new hires, some crucial conversations with existing directors and partners, and a big presentation on Monday.

This process created so much weekly anxiety, and it was only Sunday. The week had not even started yet! I began shifting a few things around and heard the echo of Stephen Covey's voice in my head telling me, "The key is not to prioritize what's on your schedule but to schedule your priorities." I leaned back on the couch and thought, *What are my priorities?*

Then the NFL game I was watching caught my eye. It was close. With a few minutes left in the third quarter, my favorite team was driving, and the camera quickly zoomed in on the offensive coordinator. The coordinator, headset on, paced the sideline, and his eyes darted back and forth between the field and a white laminated sheet in his hands. The sheet was about eleven by seventeen inches and loaded with small writing in a rainbow of colors, and it covered the mouth of the coordinator, who called the next play into his headset for the quarterback standing about twenty yards away from him.

The camera went back to the field of play. The ball was snapped. The quarterback faked a handoff to the running back (play action) and dropped back into the pocket. He looked left, pump-faked to the wide receiver on that side of the field, and then quickly pivoted and threw the ball deep down the right sideline to a wide-open receiver. *Touchdown!*

I should have been excited that my team had just scored, but I sat completely still. I'd had an epiphany. My mind rewound its mental tape to the moment prior to the play, to the offensive coordinator with the laminated sheet at his fingertips, a tool that enabled him to quickly call an effective play.

My mind was blown. As I watched more games that day, I didn't even care about the games anymore but simply watched the sidelines to see how many coaches used these sheets and how often they were using them. Quickly, it became evident this was a best practice used by every coordinator in the NFL. How had I never noticed? Every single coach I saw on TV that day had a laminated sheet of paper at the tip of their nose during every second of every possession.

I realized that all football teams and coaches have an overwhelming amount of content to study each week as they prepare for an opponent: their team Play Book, game film, player intelligence, roster diagnostics, and more. If they could put all that information on one sheet of paper, why couldn't I do that for my workweek?

PROFESSIONAL TMI

Have you ever stopped to think about how many books, podcasts, LinkedIn articles, blogs, conferences, seminars, Facebook posts, Ted Talks, and more there are on professional development? It's crazy. Business professionals spend billions of dollars for the next great piece of advice that will instantly propel them upward in their company or industry. Most of the ideas are extremely insightful and, if applied correctly, could help many improve professionally. The challenge is that there is just too much information, and many people are unable to effectively apply what they learn to their daily lives.

We are bombarded with information, and despite our best intentions, we are creatures of our old ways and unhelpful habits. When faced with a critical situation that drives anxiety or pressure, we constantly go back to our natural reaction and completely forget about what we learned or intended to try differently this time around.

For years, I was no different. Although a voracious learner, I lacked an intentional approach to implementing what I spent so many hours learning. I would show up to work armed with this new information crammed into my brain, but I never thought about how or when to apply it. Looking back, I realize that I just hoped it would naturally find its way into my style or approach. I was reactive to each meeting, situation, and day, and even worse, I failed to get a return on my invested resources.

In early 2014, as a newly married man and a junior executive at a Fortune 100 company, I wanted to improve or develop in certain areas of leadership, business, time management, and life. Now that I had moved from an individual contributor to a manager, how could I become a leader of leaders in a large organization? How could I balance my time despite having much more responsibilities, including having a team of people reporting to me? How could I do this and not jeopardize my relationships, both inside and outside the company? And most importantly, how could I accomplish this while growing a thriving family? I sought out every book, podcast, article, conference, video, and excerpt on those subjects, thinking that if I just kept learning all I could, I would improve in each area of focus.

I can recall so many times when I read a page in a book, received guidance from a mentor, or heard something that excited me so much in the moment that I knew I had the answers. There were times when I was driving to work, listening to a podcast, and heard something so impactful that I had to pull over and relisten to what I'd just heard over and over again. Sometimes I would then email myself what would turn out later to be a cryptic message with hopes of never forgetting this piece of wisdom again. Until I inevitably did.

In those "aha" moments, excited by this latest information, my mind would often float off into a daydream where I would envision myself in a situation using this newfound advice. In my professional fantasy, there I was, killing it in a presentation and being hoisted by the team in celebration. It was like the scene in A Christmas Story when the main character, Ralphie, hands in his homework assignment and starts to daydream that he's astonished his teacher with the essay's brilliance, leading to a fantastical celebration and the adoration of everyone in the room. So basically, I was handling my career like an imaginative nine year old, and something had to change.

More often than not, I would completely forget this epiphany that I pulled a motor vehicle over to relisten to. Even worse than forgetting it, I never applied it once in my professional day-to-day.

Have you experienced this in your professional journey as well? If the answer is yes, keep reading.

PROBLEM STATEMENT: COGNITIVE LOAD IS REAL

How many books about professional or leadership development do you have at your desk, in your home library, or in your Audible queue? How many conferences have you attended to help you improve in some way? Do you have a mentor or executive coach? How many times have you learned something and been extremely energized about the concept, only to forget to apply it to drive improvement? Why does this happen to so many of us? Some argue that a major reason for this is cognitive load.

Cognitive load theory is an instructional design theory that reflects the way we process information. During learning, information must be held in your working memory until it has been processed sufficiently to pass into your long-term memory. Your working memory's capacity is limited. When too much information is presented at once, your working memory becomes overwhelmed, and much of that information is lost. That leads to information overload. The law of diminishing returns applies to the amount of information you have and the effectiveness or accuracy of the decision you will make.

The well-known New York City marketer and writer Oksana Tunikova defines information overload as:

> the state of feeling overwhelmed by the volume of information to the point at which one feels more confused than knowledgeable about a particular topic. Information overload can manifest itself as brain fog and difficulty making decisions. In general, information overload is the kind of stress you feel when you consume more information than you can "digest" (and more than it is needed to make a decision).[1]

In researching cognitive load for this book, I ironically faced information overload. There are even prescribed names for this problem: infoxication, infobesity, data smog, and more. Regardless of the name, this is a problem for many people—especially business professionals—whether they admit it or not.

Information overload makes it difficult to decipher which concepts are useful and which are garbage. In addition to proactively pulling information, we are passively bombarded with it every second. I bet you've gotten three to four

1   Oksana Tunikova, "Are We Consuming Too Much Information?," Medium, June 7, 2018, https://medium.com/@tunikova/are-we-consuming-too-much-information-b68f62500089.

notifications on your phone since you started this chapter. We are paralyzed by the amount of information at our fingertips, and most of us lack the time to sort through all of it to not only determine what information will be useful but also quickly recall and apply it to our situation.

Another expert in the field of information overload and its impact on decision-making is Peter Gordon Roetzel, a professor of accounting and information systems. In 2018, Roetzel published his research, "Information Overload in the Information Age." In the work, Roetzel discusses the deterioration of good decision-making at and beyond a person's information overload threshold, or when too much information affects a person's ability to make good decisions.

Roetzel's research suggests we all have:

A critical point that as information loads approach the point at which they can no longer be processed effectively (for whatever reason), decision-making performance begins to deteriorate. This change in performance occurs because the decision-maker is able to process less and less of the total information available to help make good decisions. In other words, imagine a scenario in which making the right choice requires an executive to process ten pieces of information, the maximum amount manageable by this particular leader. Suddenly, because of a competitor's major innovation, the necessary information load increases from ten to twenty pieces. In this case, the decision-maker who was maxed out at ten analytical tasks (100%) is forced to shift and make a decision at only 50% capacity. As the required information count climbs higher, the processing capacity percentage drops, thus generating a greater probability of making a bad choice.[2]

To help you determine the point at which too much information will start to impact your decision-making effectiveness, it is important that we unpack the causes of information overload. The following diagram, from Kazi Mostak Gausul Hoq, an associate professor in the Department of Information Science and Library Management at the University of Dhaka, highlights the most common causes of information overload.

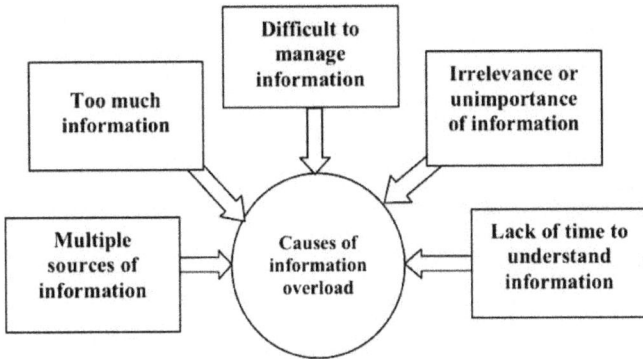

---

2   Carlos Alvarenga, "Information Rich, Attention Poor: The Danger of Information Overload," *Thematiks: A Business Research Digital Journal* (November 2, 2022), https://www.thematiks.com/p/information-rich-attention-poor-the.

The diagram is from Hoq's study, "Information Overload: Causes, Consequences, and Remedies."[3] The study stressed the importance of developing techniques and technologies to counter the effects of information overload.

I struggled for years to find a solution, technique, or framework to combat information overload and likely missed chances to make the best decisions in crucial moments. Then, on that fateful Sunday, I saw that seventeen-by-eleven-inch laminated sheet of paper. Seeing it would change my approach to professional development and allow me to finally start preventing the causes of information overload that had previously curbed my professional growth.

As business professionals, we may not have a week, or even hours, to prepare for one game like football coaching staffs do, but could we build a repository for all our learnings and develop a game plan of what we wanted to implement and execute week in and week out? Could we create an at-a-glance reminder sheet to help each day as situations, meetings, or deliverables arose? How intentional were our weekly improvement routines, and how much better were we all really at getting at the skills we said we would improve year after year?

Coaches have made an art out of organizing, recalling, and applying data and information in critical moments. Whether

---

3   Kazi Mostak Gausul Hoq, "Information Overload: Causes, Consequences and Remedies—A Study," *Philosophy and Progress* 55, no. 1–2 (February 2016): 49, https://doi.org/10.3329/pp.v55i1-2.26390.

you are a football fan or not, I challenge you to watch a football game someday and notice how every single coordinator or play-calling coach on the sideline is equipped with a laminated sheet of paper. These routines and artifacts are standard in the football world. I believe the Play Sheet could be the standard in the professional world and could help many get ahead of the curve in their preparation and secure an advantage to succeed in each professional season.

MY JOURNEY TO LEARN THE ART OF FOOTBALL COACHING

How does a corporate executive like me know that a Play Sheet can make the move from the football field to the boardroom to help you dominate against your competitors? Well, after I had my Sunday afternoon epiphany, I immediately built my very own personalized Play Sheet to use in my day-to-day job, and it worked. I will discuss the process of creating a Play Sheet for your professional arena in the chapters ahead.

After years of using my own Play Sheet and being asked by colleagues and mentees how to create one, I thought maybe it could actually be of use to others. When I initially created this tool, I was not sure what it was called or how coaches built theirs. I simply put my thoughts down on one sheet and used them in my day-to-day work life. But would that process be repeatable for anyone?

If this concept was going to work, I needed to do some research and talk to the experts.

Now, I might be five foot nine (okay, five foot eight) and a hundred and nothing pounds, but I do have some football roots. My path in life has unexpectedly followed the trail of some of the most notable football people and programs in history.

I went to high school at St. Thomas Aquinas in Fort Lauderdale, Florida. In 2005, *Sports Illustrated* recognized the school as having the third-best athletics program in the country, and it has only become stronger since. The football team in particular has won fifteen state championships—ten in the last twelve years, and a Florida-state-record five in a row. Also, they have won three national high school football titles since 2010, according to MaxPreps. In 2020, St. Thomas claimed more active NFL players than any high school in the nation, with eleven. The next closest school had six.

Notable alumni include Brian Piccolo, Michael Irvin, the Bosa brothers (Joey and Nick), James White, Geno Atkins, Giovani Bernard, Phillip Dorsett, and Lamarcus Joyner. For several years, former NFL star Jason Taylor was the defensive coordinator at St. Thomas under the incredible leadership of Coach Roger Harriott and, until his retirement, the heralded athletic director George Smith.

For undergraduate study, I went to Valdosta State University (VSU). The success of the high school and university teams in the small town of Valdosta, Georgia, drove ESPN to dub it Titletown USA. I was a golfer at VSU, and the pride in local teams was something I felt as a student and as an athlete.

Valdosta High School holds the record for most wins of any football program in the US, and Netflix aired a series called *Titletown High* about the school and the football program. In addition to the success of the high school program, the Valdosta State football program has become its own powerhouse over the last two decades. Since 2004, Valdosta State has been to six and won four NCAA Division II national championships and has been a successful development pool for outstanding coaches. Some notable coaches with VSU on their résumés are Hal Mumme, Chris Hatcher, David Dean, Mike Leach, Kirby Smart, and Will Muschamp. In 2020, Leach (Mississippi State), Smart (Georgia), and Muschamp (South Carolina) were all head coaches in the Southeastern Conference (SEC). Kirby Smart led the Georgia Bulldogs to back-to-back College Football Playoff National Championships in 2021 and 2022.

Lastly, I got my MBA at Georgia Tech in Atlanta and worked as a graduate assistant for the athletics program. While there, I got to briefly see the brilliance of athletic director Dan Radakovich. Dan went on to be the AD at Clemson from 2013 to 2021, and under his leadership Clemson won two football national championships.

In 2010, after graduating, I moved to San Antonio, Texas, for work. In Florida, football was a massive system that always seemed like a machine to me, but football in Texas is like religion—it's almost spiritual. Friday night lights were just bigger and brighter in Texas, and I loved it.

Even though I opted to become a corporate drone instead of an athletic director or a coach, I did still have various connections to coaches and people in their professional world. I made some calls (a lot of calls) and drafted some emails, and before I knew it, I was interviewing coaches at multiple league levels and positions across the country. Several referred me to the American Football Coaches Association (AFCA), and I immediately googled the organization. At the top of its website was a banner promoting the annual AFCA convention in a few weeks—in San Antonio. My heart skipped a beat, and I felt like a kid whose parents had just told him that they were headed to Disney World.

At this point it was January of 2019, and there were hundreds—thousands—of high school and college football coaches in one convention center ten minutes from my house. My mission on that day and in the months ahead was to learn all the secrets, best practices, and innovative concepts of every football coach who would talk to me. Over a two-year period, with a global pandemic in the middle, I interviewed everyone I could. I attended several Texas High School Coaches Association (THSCA) and AFCA conferences, did in-person and Zoom interviews, and continued to build a network of coaches who could help me improve my process of recording, retaining, and recalling information and ideas and apply them to my business interactions.

Most importantly, I wanted to learn the processes used to create Play Sheets as well as how they are used and how they have changed over time. How did coaches condense the overwhelming amount of information at their disposal each week to one sheet and successfully use it in high-pressure situations, allowing them to win? I wanted to see how the process I had created could be improved, and I wanted to validate my hypothesis that my Play Sheet could be a universal tool to help professionals achieve success in their careers.

The coaches I spoke with approached (sometimes tentatively) my questions with an open mind, sharing their approach and best practices. It's my honor to share what I learned from them with you. (For a roster of those who shared their time and experiences, please see the Acknowledgments section at the end of the book.)

WHAT YOU'LL LEARN

The collegiate and professional sports worlds have figured out how to solve the problem of overload, and now, with *The Play Sheet*, professionals can learn to apply a simple, at-a-glance system to their own careers.

Like a football game, this book is divided into four quarters:

1. **First Quarter: Ethos**. Establish your ethos, objectives, and key results to create guardrails to filter what is worthy enough to spend time learning and developing.

2. **Second Quarter: Play Book**. Record, aggregate, and organize information in one place to quickly access or reference key concepts and plays.

3. **Third Quarter: Play Sheet**. Use your plays based on the situation at hand to help you execute more effectively and achieve more professional wins.

4. **Fourth Quarter: Adjust**. Establish a cadence of retrospectives to continuously adjust your categories and plays as you master skills or your external factors shift.

Before you build your Play Book and Play Sheet and before you continue learning anything, the first phase is to determine who you want to be and define your personal ethos and development objectives.

Next, you'll inventory and consolidate all your quotes, concepts, one-liners, ideas, and so on into one repository—your Play Book. I will help you organize your Play Book so it can be an easy-to-navigate resource for you to pull plays from as you build your Play Sheet.

Then you will build your Play Sheet and learn how to effectively use it over time and in high-pressure situations. Finally, you will discover how to build repeatable routines to make adjustments to your Play Sheet as you continue your process of professional growth.

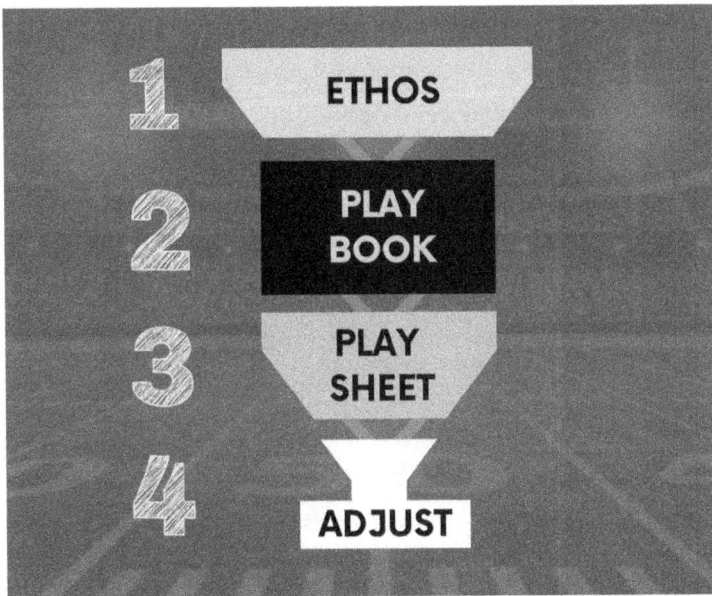

I have read books and found professional plays that I added to my repertoire, but prior to borrowing these coaches' best practices to build a framework, I had never intentionally evaluated the situation at hand, evaluated the plays in my Play Book, added a play to my Play Sheet, and then executed it intentionally in a critical situation. Now that I have, I will never be without that laminated sheet in a game-day situation. And I don't think you should either.

Most business professionals are not intentional with their development or preparation. Many react to whatever "fire drill" or "priority meeting" comes their way each week. While we'll develop your own repeatable routines to master your ability to execute with excellence in your day-to-day, each chapter will simultaneously share a glimpse into the brilliance and simplicity of how most football coaches, their staffs, and their teams build a culture, build a Play Book, prepare for their immediate opponent, build and use their Play Sheet, and make adjustments.

Many of us see coaches pacing the sideline on game day, but we do not see what they do prior to game day or prior to the season. Their preparation, routines, and frameworks help them build culture, develop a system, and find the right play for the right situation. After studying coaches, I know their common best practices can translate to the business world and help you in your very own professional development. Lastly, in case you are unfamiliar with some of the football terminology in the book, don't be intimidated. Please search "Glossary of American football terms" on Wikipedia to help you as needed.

Once you understand the coaches' approach, you will understand the value of their preparation, repeatable routines, and simple frameworks, and you will hopefully be more likely to develop your own personalized system that will allow you to unlock your potential and achieve more consistent success.

PREGAME RECAP

1. Many business professionals spend countless hours learning how to improve themselves, but most fall short when it comes to organizing, recalling, and applying what they learned into their day-to-day work.

2. Your working memory's capacity is limited. When too much information is presented at once, it becomes overwhelming, and much of that information is lost. That leads to the concept of information overload.

3. To avoid information overload and aid in the recall and application of concepts learned during personal and professional development, create a one-page Play Sheet designed around those used by football coaches at all levels. In four phases, this book will show you how to do so.

FIRST QUARTER

WHO ARE YOU AND WHO DO YOU WANT TO BE?

"Culture and tradition are contributing factors to our holistic success."

—COACH ROGER HARRIOTT

FILM STUDY

THE IMPORTANCE OF TEAM ETHOS

I interviewed Coach Darrell Andrus, a high school football coach for nineteen years in South Texas. As of this writing, Coach Andrus works at Jourdanton High School, and I asked him about his team culture, ethos, and mission. Like many others, he immediately said these were vital to his team. At Jourdanton you will see the number 212 throughout the team's Play Book, "212" stickers on helmets, and "212" posters in the locker room; if you played there, you understand the concept of 212. Coach Andrus leveraged this from Sam Parker and Mac Anderson's book *212: The Extra Degree*. Parker and Anderson's concept starts with the fact that at 211 degrees Fahrenheit, water is very hot, but at 212 degrees, it boils. The extra degree creates change, makes steam, and can power something as strong as a train.

Coach Andrus described a time a few years back when their opponent was breaking toward the end zone off an interception return. His fullback could have just thrown his hands down in frustration, but the 212 concept was embedded in him, and he immediately chased the opposing defensive back heading for the end zone. The Jourdanton fullback caught up with the opposing player just in time and punched the ball out before it crossed the goal line. The ball went through the end zone, and instead of a touch*down* for the opponent, the play resulted in a touch*back* and no points for the other team. The entire sideline erupted and screamed, "212! 212! 212!" That extra effort and making that play at the one-yard line saved Jourdanton's confidence and shifted its momentum not only in that game but for the remainder of the season. Also, it was a shining example for others to follow this ethos.

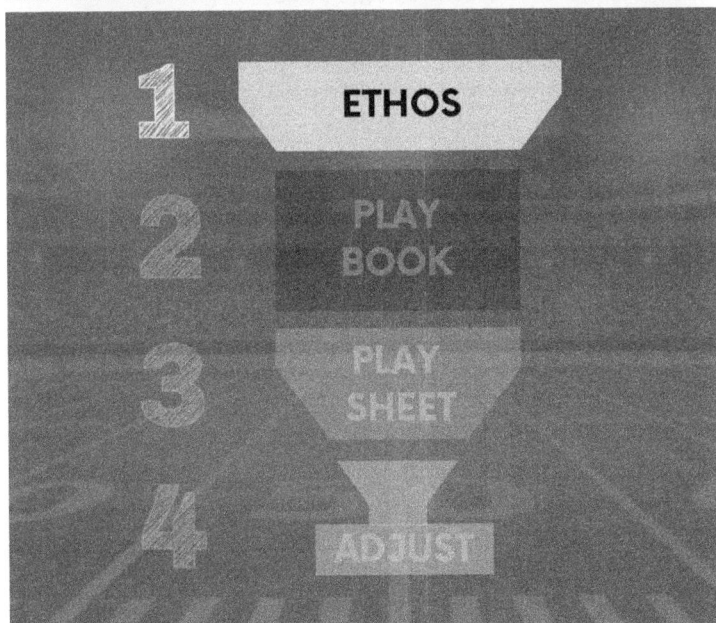

DEFINE YOUR ETHOS, OBJECTIVES, AND KEY RESULTS

Many people are curious and lifelong learners, but as you read in the introduction, too much information or irrelevant information can increase cognitive load. People always want to cut the corner and jump right into creating their Play Book and Play Sheet. That approach is a big mistake.

Those steps and the associated artifacts are critical, but they are only as good as the foundation they are set upon. Jumping into them right away is an activity trap that might feel productive but will lead to less effective results because you did not put a filter on the information you consumed or the concepts you attempted to execute. The end goal is for you to execute effective plays in your day-to-day like a coach does in each game, but to successfully achieve this future state, you must first *define (in the context of your professional life) who you are today and who you want to be in the future.* Try not to cheat yourself; dedicate some time to thoughtfully completing the following steps.

- **Define**: Before you continue learning anything, determine *who you want to be*, and define your personal ethos.

- **Analyze**: Evaluate your current state, identifying strengths and opportunities. Assess *strengths and gaps* in your skills that align with your desired state. Then *prioritize* them.

- **Document**: Set and write down your development objectives and key results (OKRs) to track progress over time.

Once you complete these initial steps, I will summarize how to apply and use these guardrails to "filter" what is worth learning and worthy of space on your Play Book and Play Sheet.

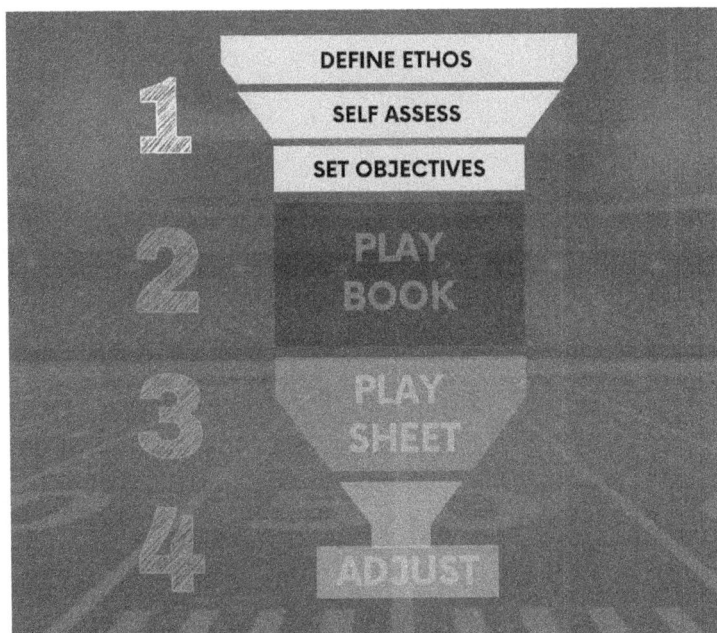

STEP 1: DEFINE YOUR ETHOS

Coaches Start with Ethos and Culture

In my observations and conversations with coaches across the country, one thing was constant: all of them stressed the importance of building a team mission and ethos. Coaches at all levels validated that establishing these concepts first was the foundation to building a successful program and team.

Ethos means "character" in Greek, but today many define it as the practices or values that distinguish one person, organization, or society from others. There are hundreds of football programs in the country, and in such a crowded landscape, coaches must differentiate their programs and determine what makes them unique, different, or desirable. Open any coach's Play Book, and you will immediately see that program's mission and ethos.

University of Texas at San Antonio:
The Triangle of Toughness

Around the same time that I moved to San Antonio in 2010, a football program was established at the University of Texas at San Antonio. The team had some great seasons early on, but in 2019 they hired Coach Jeff Traylor. Anyone in the 210 area code can tell you that in his first three years, the energy and success of the team skyrocketed. There are many reasons for the team's back-to-back Conference USA championships and top-twenty-five rankings, but every time coach Traylor, his staff, or his players are asked about their program, they always bring it back to their team ethos, the Triangle of Toughness. In interviews, Traylor has stated, "It's all we talk about, preach, and try to live by. It is our brand."

Traylor and his staff use this concept to reinforce their mission and values. Words bordering the middle triangle represent the team's three units: special teams, offense, and defense. Bordering those triangles are the phrases "Selfless Perfect Effort," "Integrity, Passion," and "Mental & Physical Toughness."

St. Thomas Aquinas: The Standard and You Go, We Go

Another mission and ethos are from my high school alma mater, St. Thomas Aquinas in Fort Lauderdale, Florida. If you are not familiar with St. Thomas Aquinas, refer back to the introduction for my (slightly biased) paragraphs on the team's accomplishments under the coaching tenure of Roger Harriott and George Smith.

Here is a snippet of the football packet the coaches handed out to all players, coaches, and families at the start of the 2022 season. The document shows the team motto or ethos: "You Go, We Go." In the packet there are other key cultural elements established in the program's statement document.

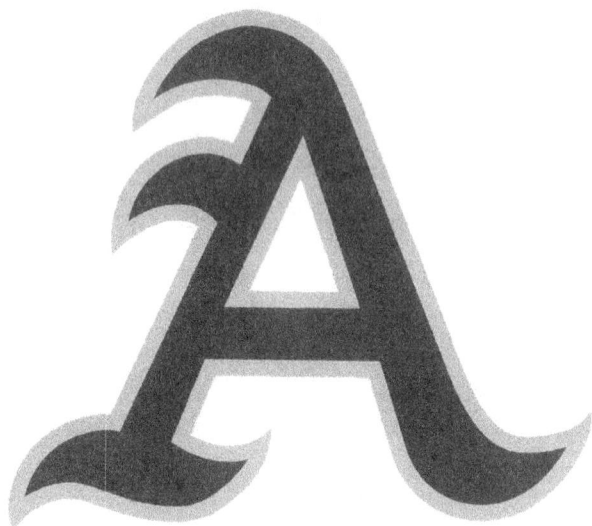

SUMMER 2022

MAKE A STATEMENT

"Grant me, O Lord my God, a mind to know you, a heart to seek you, wisdom to find you, conduct pleasing to you, faithful perseverance in waiting for you, and a hope of finally embracing you. Amen."
—Saint Thomas Aquinas

YOU GO, WE GO

NATIONAL CHAMPIONS
2008, 2010, 2019

STATE CHAMPIONS
1992, 1997, 1999, 2007, 2008, 2010, 2012, 2014, 2015, 2016, 2019, 2020, 2021

STATEMENT

5/31/22: Raider Night

- Standard: Faith, Family, Tradition, and Excellence
- Motto: You Go, We Go
- Aquinas Expectation: Hold the Rope
- 2022 Team Theme: TBA
- Message: Football is our ministry to develop efficient interpersonal skills and in interdependent culture—we are life coaches.
- Philosophy: To cultivate a family-oriented, first-class, productive, and successful ministry-based experience.
- Mission: To be servant leaders of God and productive citizens of society.
- Forces: Great things happen for good people who are devoted to the greater good.
  - Golden Rule: "Treat others how you want to be treated."

Professional Frameworks Suggest Starting with a Mission or Ethos

Like many great football coaches, some of the best executive coaches and leadership authors have stressed the importance of setting a mission or ethos. In his book *The 7 Habits of Highly Effective People*, Stephen Covey discusses a habit called begin with the end in mind:

To begin with the end in mind means to start with clear understanding of your destination. It means to know where you are going so that you better understand where you are now and so that the steps you take are always in the right direction.[4]

Over the last decade, my area of professional expertise has been portfolio management and agile transformation. My teams and I have led IT project portfolios as large as $400 million at Fortune 100 companies. In my tenure as a portfolio management executive, I held multiple positions where portfolios had previously struggled to deliver business or customer value. Many times, after my team and I performed analysis on the portfolio's health, we would determine most projects, and the dollars and resources allocated to them, were not aligned to the company's or division's strategic objectives. Here are some recently published statistics from Gartner about the lack of strategic alignment to project delivery that suggest this is a problem in many organizations:

- 60% of organizations do not link their budgets to their corporate strategy.

---

4   Stephen R. Covey, *The 7 Habits of Highly Effective People: Powerful Lessons in Personal Change* (New York: Free Press, 1989), 98.

- 95% of the delivery workforce does not understand their company's strategy.
- 61% of executives struggle to bridge the gap between strategy formulation and implementation.

I have learned in my career that poor portfolio health is often driven by a lack of alignment between strategy and execution. To counter this problem, I often brought together strategy teams, executives, and key stakeholders to conduct a simple yet effective SAFe (Scaled Agile Framework) exercise from the SAFe Play Book. I would collaborate with these partners to create a portfolio vision. According to the SAFe Play Book:

> The portfolio vision sets a longer-term context for near-term decisions in a way that is both practical and inspirational, clearly articulating why the future state is something worth achieving. Understanding the longer-term view helps make more informed choices about the development of functionality in both the short and long run.[5]

Coaches, companies, and project portfolios all focus on a clear future state grounded in their culture, values, beliefs, and aspirations. And those that lack that clarity of destination

---

5   SAFe Studio, "Portfolio Vision," Scaled Agile Inc., updated October 12, 2023, https://scaledagileframework.com/portfolio-vision.

often find themselves busy yet ineffective at delivering long-term results.

So as I started building this framework, I assessed how aligned my professional development was to my ethos and desired future state. Even though I practiced these principles frequently in my profession, my self-assessment made me realize that I was rarely following this framework when it came to my professional and personal development. In reality, I was not remotely intentional in my approach and was often reactive in my effort to improve. Whatever concept popped into my social feeds would grab my attention. I would consume it and go forward with the hope that I would magically master that skill or concept.

To this point, I had never used anything to filter what I spent time learning or consuming and definitely did not consider it from the perspective of my personal ethos or desired future-state objectives. As a result, I was ineffective in delivering or executing the concepts I spent so much time and energy consuming. Nothing was intentional or aligned to the strategic goals of my career. After talking to the coaches, I realized I was a hypocrite. For some reason, I would coach my team and others at work daily to follow these principles, but I never applied them to my own professional development.

After this epiphany, I decided to finally follow the advice of Covey, these coaches, and the teachings of SAFe. I decided to slow down, take a step back, and ask myself, *Who am I today, and who do I want to be in the future?* I paused learning any new concepts, building out my Play Book and Play Sheet, and making any attempts to implement new skills into my day-to-day work life. I focused on driving clarity on my personal ethos, my desired objectives, and my ultimate destination.

It was a game changer and brought home Covey's words: "How different our lives are when we really know what is deeply important to us, and, keeping that picture in mind, we manage ourselves each day to be and to do what really matters most."[6]

Now let me help you do the same.

How to Develop Your Personal Ethos

Take a look at the image on the following page. The road you take to get from today to your desired destination five-plus years from now may have many twists and turns for a variety of reasons, but let's begin with the end in mind and ground ourselves in our values and beliefs and who we ultimately want to be in the future.

Here are some coaching tips on how to develop your personal ethos statement:

1. Remember that the purpose of this ethos is to provide direction and inform your actions.

6 Covey, *The 7 Habits of Highly Effective People*, 98.

5+ years
04

3-5 years
03

1-3 years
02

Today
01

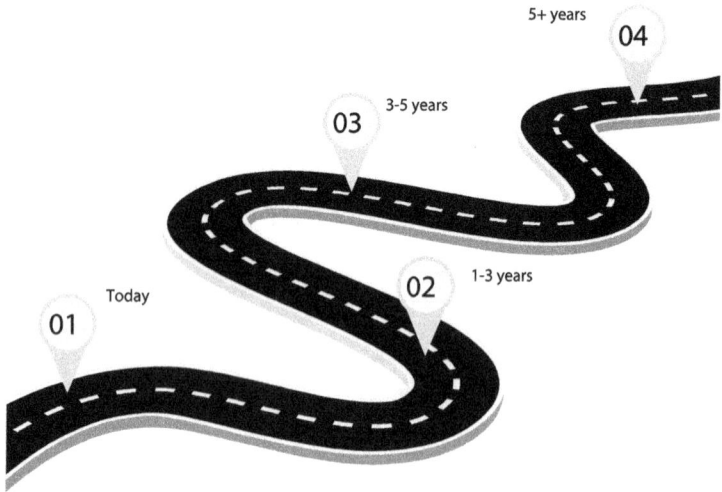

2. Dedicate time to complete this exercise. It requires deep reflection and should take several drafts to complete.

3. Do this in a quiet place or a place that brings you fulfillment or joy.

4. Center your ethos statement around your core values and beliefs.

5. Make it aspirational and motivational yet realistic.

6. Be specific.

7. Make it long-lasting. This should not be a fluid, constantly changing statement.

8. It should focus on who you want to be and what you want to do.

9. Do not worry about the length of your ethos statement. It can be one word or a few paragraphs.

10. Have fun with it. Maybe make it a logo, like the Triangle of Toughness, or anything that helps.

Now that you have your instructions, use the clipboard (or any source of your choosing), and write your personal ethos statement. As you complete this step, please note this is not easy, and it will take time. Once you complete this exercise, you are ready for the next step. To assist in this exercise, here is a detailed example of the intent and mission behind the "You Go, We Go" ethos from the football coaches at St. Thomas Aquinas High School.

> The St. Thomas Aquinas (STA) football program strives to create a faith based environment conducive to academic, athletic, and social development for our players. We are committed to providing a comprehensive, safe, and effective interscholastic football program based upon Godly principles and the needs of our players. The St. Thomas Aquinas football program parallels our school belief and goals with the chief mission of St. Thomas Aquinas at heart. The St. Thomas Aquinas football staff is devoted to providing servant leadership, resources, and guidance to ensure that all players are given the finest experience possible. Each STA coach is issued a direct objective to support our players' intercollegiate and career aspirations, as well as promote healthy lifestyle habits. Ultimately, our goal is to cultivate a

first-class environment that exemplifies an authentic sense of school spirit and pride as a St. Thomas Aquinas Raider.[7]

7   Roger Harriot (head coach, Thomas Aquinas High School football program), email exchange with the author, March 25, 2021.

STEP 2: CONDUCT A GAP ANALYSIS BETWEEN YOUR CURRENT AND FUTURE STATES

In the last exercise, you envisioned your future state and drafted your personal ethos statement. Now go back to the roadmap figure and focus on your current state, location pin 1. The distance between 1 and 4 on the roadmap represents how far you have to travel to achieve your future state. For example, in 2010 the Auburn Play Book included the goal of becoming the number-one offense in the country. In 2010 they were the seventh-ranked offense, so when the coaching staff came back in 2011, they had a sharp vision to go from seventh to first to achieve their mission.

A simple technique to develop a game plan on how to move from current state to future state is a SWOT analysis. SWOT stands for strengths, weaknesses, opportunities, and threats. For the purpose of our exercise, we will only focus on your strengths and weaknesses. You have been asked this question in any interview you have ever been in, but I need you to be honest with yourself here. What are your true strengths, and what are your areas that need improvement?

When football coaches prepare for their next opponent, they conduct a similar analysis. Coaches break down or cut film from previous games or seasons to analyze the strengths and weaknesses of their opponents. Coaches organize the film into the following categories to find tendencies:

- Down and distance (first and ten, third and short)
- Run-pass option (RPO)
- Formations (I formation, T formation)
- Possession (first possession of game)
- Personnel packages (one running back, one tight end)
- What hash mark the play started from (start in center of field, right side of field)

For example, they may notice that an opposing coach called one type of run a certain percentage of the time in the last four games. They will quickly identify that as one of the opposing team's strengths. They continue doing this to find the meat of what the opponent does often and identify the top five to ten runs that team consistently runs. These coaches are looking for tells, as in a poker game, through the data, or film. The likelihood of the opposing team running a particular play is high; therefore, the coaches should flag it and devise how they will plan against it. The output is a tendency stat sheet, which is a summary of the opposing team's stats at a glance that allows coaches to see what type of call the opposing team makes most often, organized by down and distance, personnel, formation, and so on.

The following shows a defensive coordinator's stat sheet, which gives the down and distance tendencies of an opponent they were preparing for that week.

Down & Distance				
	Runs		Passes	
P & 10	25	65%	14	35%
1st & 10	42	70%	18	30%
2nd & 1-3	4	100%	0	0%
2nd & 4-6	8	50%	8	50%
2nd & 7+	24	50%	25	50%
3rd & 1-3	10	90%	1	10%
3rd & 4-6	7	65%	4	35%
3rd & 7+	3	12%	22	88%
4th Down	0	0%	2	100%
Totals	123	57%	94	43%

Personnel				
	Plays	Runs	Pass	Tendency
11 Personnel	149	85	64	57% RUN
10 Personnel	33	7	26	80% PASS
12 Personnel	30	27	3	90% RUN
00 Personnel	2	1	1	50% R/P

Formation				
	Plays	Runs	Pass	Tendency
Trey	38	23	18	55% RUN
Trey Hvy Buck	32	22	10	70% RUN
Dbls Hvy Buck	20	13	7	65% RUN
Trips	18	8	10	55% PASS
Trio	17	2	15	90% PASS
Dbls Wing	12	11	1	90% RUN

They know that 100 percent of the time the opposing team has run when it is second down and less than three yards to go so far this season, so they may prepare accordingly to stuff the run if it is second and short when they are on defense. Coach Dom Anderson, defensive coordinator and linebackers coach at Fayetteville State University, told me multiple times, "Everyone has a tendency; you just need to find it and expose it."

Coach Anderson and other coaches are prioritizing. They leverage the tendency data to focus where they spend their time and energy preparing for the upcoming opponent. They focus on the big picture and strategic themes. They do not consume their time or resources by mastering the one-offs.

Most coaches play to their strengths and play to their opponents' weaknesses. This is where they devote hours of film study each week, so I am asking you to roll back the film on yourself to prepare a game plan. Please fill out the following template.

STRENGTHS	WEAKNESSES

Most professionals focus only on one side of the ball here: the opportunities. But I suggest you build plays in your Play Book and on your Play Sheet for each area of your professional development.

Next, let us assess how relevant each strength and each weakness is for you to embody your ethos and achieve your goals. Take the comprehensive list and prioritize the items based on how important each skill is to achieving your future state.

In portfolio management, agile transformation, and strategic planning, prioritization is a difficult exercise for companies to perform effectively. David Allen once said, "You can do anything but not everything." Organizations and individuals struggle with doing the most meaningful and impactful work first versus trying to execute too many things at once.

Here is an example of one of my personal prioritized lists from back in 2017 and a blank list for you to use to complete the exercise. As you can see, I balanced improving on both strengths and weaknesses. They all cannot be number one, and there are no ties, so please rank them in priority order.

Example:

COMBINED LIST OF STRENGTHS AND WEAKNESSES	
1	**OPPORTUNITY:** TIME MANAGEMENT / WORK AND LIFE BALANCE
2	**OPPORTUNITY:** EXECUTIVE LEVEL COMMUNICATION
3	**STRENGTH:** RELATIONSHIP BUILDING / NETWORKING (CONTINUE THIS STRENGTH)
4	**STRENGTH:** LEADERSHIP (LEAD AT HIGHER AND BROADER LEVEL)
5	**OPPORTUNITY:** MINDFULNESS

Template for You to Complete:

	COMBINED LIST OF STRENGTHS AND WEAKNESSES
1	
2	
3	
4	
5	
6	
7	
8	
9	
10	

Now that you have your strengths and weaknesses in order, rate your maturity with each strength or weakness from 1 to 10, with 1 being very poor (you would fail the class on this topic) and 10 being subject matter expert (you should teach the master class on this topic).

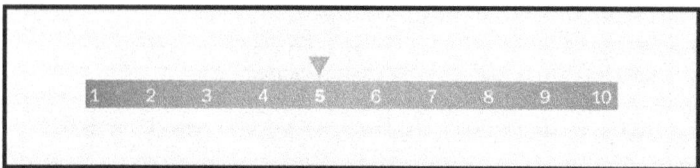

| 1 | 2 | 3 | 4 | 5 | 6 | 7 | 8 | 9 | 10 |

Now that you have prioritized each area according to its alignment with your desired outcomes and rated your maturity in each area, you have a view similar to the coaches' at-a-glance tendency sheet. As you continue your development journey, this view will help you quickly recognize whether the information you are about to learn or consume is a priority or a nice to have. If it is an outlier and not a priority, then it may not be worth your time. If what you are thinking about learning or developing is aligned to your ethos and this priority list, then you have validated that this is a good investment of your time and energy.

Next, you will define what, specifically, you hope to achieve in your development journey so you can continue to measure your progress over time.

STEP 3: DEVELOP YOUR PROFESSIONAL DEVELOPMENT OBJECTIVES AND KEY RESULTS

Most coaches have key performance metrics for each game. After the game, they grade the overall team on how they did against those objectives. This evaluation also gives them quick insight into what they need to continue coaching on or where they are starting to improve in certain areas of their team. As an example, an offensive coordinator may set an objective to have less than one turnover or fewer than three holding calls in a game. If they meet these goals, that is a win for the offense. If not, they may have to coach harder in those areas that indicate opportunity as an offense.

Many technology firms over the last two decades have adopted the use of objectives and key results (OKRs) to "provide a simple approach to create alignment and engagement around measurable and ambitious goals," according to Felipe Castro, the author of *The Beginner's Guide to OKR*.[8] There are entire books written on how to develop and use OKRs, and this section will hopefully simplify the concept and teach you how to write some for your own ambitious and aspirational goals.

Creating OKRs is just as important as writing your ethos because they will provide a measurable way to determine whether you are progressing in your development. They will help you to constantly reflect on the big picture and will connect your overall strategy to your day-to-day development efforts.

- O is for objective: This is what you want to do and where you want to go.
- KR is for key results: These are quantifiable targets to measure the success of the objective. There are usually three to five KRs for each O.

Here is an example from Scaled Agile of what OKRs look like.

---

8   Felipe Castro, "What is OKR?," Felipe Castro, accessed February 13, 2024, https://felipecastro.com/en/okr/what-is-okr.

OBJECTIVE	KEY RESULT
Achieve a dominant position within the autonomous delivery market	Increase serviceable market to 75% within 18 months
	Increase Net Promoter Score from 35 to 60
	Improve repeat business rates from 60% to 80%
	Acquire 15% new customers over the next 12 months

Here are some quick tips for writing your OKRs:

- Objectives should be:
  - Aspirational
  - Clear, specific, and aligned to your ethos
  - Limited to three to five at a time
  - Words, not numbers

- Key results should be:
  - Limited to three to five per objective
  - Outcomes, not tasks or activities
  - Measurable and time bound
  - Helpful in answering the question: are we achieving the objective?

Using these examples and tips, let's create your professional development OKRs. Create a minimum of three but no more than five objectives aligned to achieving your desired future state. I recommend having your ethos statement and your prioritized list of strengths and weaknesses in front of you. Your objectives should be grounded in improving those top-ranked items. For example, my top item when I assessed my strengths and weaknesses was time management. An objective for me could have been "Achieve a better balance between work, home, and health." This again will take some time, so do not rush it. When you feel your OKRs are in a good place, you are ready for the next step. Remember do not loaf or cut corners here. This is a foundational part of your long-term effectiveness.

OBJECTIVE	KEY RESULT

How to Apply and Use Your Ethos Statement and OKRs

Congratulations! I admit that these are not the most fun parts of this framework, but they are foundational and vital to your long-term results. You now have a sense of who you are today and who you want to be in the future. You are equipped with personalized criteria to provide direction and a filter in your development.

You have the basic direction from which you set your long- and short-term goals. You have the power of a written constitution based on correct principles against which every decision concerning the most effective use of your time, talents, and energies can be effectively measured.

Now that you have your ethos statement and OKRs, you will use these to filter what information you spend time learning and where you spend your energy. In the coming days, you may see an interesting article or see a business book on the *New York Times* Best Seller list, but before you consider investing time into reading it, you need to pull out your artifacts from the first three steps of this chapter and ask yourself if this is aligned to your destination. If the answer is no, you can put it in the parking lot for another time, like the coaches do with their tendency filter. Now you can invest that time into learning something relevant to your strategic themes and areas of focus.

FIRST-QUARTER HIGHLIGHTS

Through the first three steps of this chapter, you successfully mitigated two major causes of information overload. The refinement of your ethos statement, strengths and opportunities, and objectives and key results helped you filter out extraneous information and start to eliminate any concepts that are irrelevant or not important to achieving your predetermined goals.

You created the guardrails and a filter for your continuous learning and development:

- You can do anything but not everything, so you determined who you want to be and defined your personal ethos.

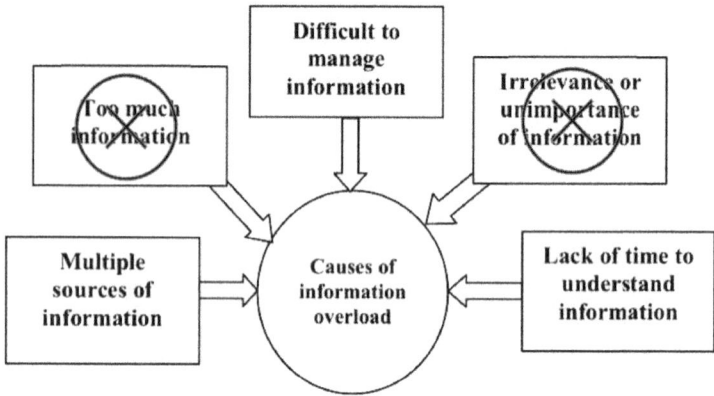

- You determined your strengths and areas that need improvement. These allow you to identify areas of professional development that will make up sections of your Play Book. Most professionals focus only on one or the other, but I suggest you build plays in your Play Book that allow you to refine your strengths and improve your weaknesses.

- You defined your objectives and key results. These objectives should clearly align with or map to your strategy or vision. You developed a few measurable key results for each objective. Objectives and key results provide a simple approach to create alignment and engagement around measurable and ambitious goals.

- As you seek more knowledge, ask yourself, *Is this relevant to my ethos and objectives?* If yes, continue; if no, add it to your reading backlog for another time.

In summary, you created your inside cover or page one of your Play Book, which will set the tone and direction for your professional development, Play Book, and Play Sheet. You or anyone else could read this page and quickly grasp your unique spirit and culture, the direction in which you are heading, and the person you aspire to be. With this ethos and clarity of direction in mind, you are now ready to create your Play Book.

THE PLAY BOOK

"Every coach needs to have a solid foundation on which their team can stand."

—COACH CHARLES BRUCE

FILM STUDY

COACH TONY ELLIOTT ADDS TO HIS PLAY BOOK

In early 2021, I interviewed Clemson University's then-offensive coordinator, Tony Elliott. At the end of that year, the University of Virginia hired Coach Elliott to be their head football coach. Under Coach Elliott's leadership as offensive coordinator, Clemson went to four College Football Playoff National Championships and won two of them. In our conversation, I asked him to tell me about a time when he and his staff found a tendency or vulnerability in an opponent in their weekly film studies that led to a successful outcome in a game.

One week back in 2016, Coach Elliott and his staff were preparing for a game against Virginia Tech, and they noticed a play that Virginia Tech had repeatedly run well against multiple opponents. It was a play-action pass where the quarterback fakes the ball to the running back and that same running back immediately curls around the offensive line and runs a few yards downfield. In the film, Coach Elliott saw that most of the defenses were fooled by the run, and their linebackers overpursued and rushed into the backfield to make a tackle on a running play. This gave the running back a chance to slip behind the linebackers to a soft spot just below the safety downfield.

After seeing this play, Coach Elliott and his staff added it to their own Play Book. "We borrowed that play, and we put it into our piggy bank for when we needed it," he said. All Coach Elliott did here was he saw a best practice of a team that played all the same opponents that Clemson did, year in and year out, and said, "If this play works so well for them, then we should add it to our inventory of plays." He said the team ran it a few times that year. They even ran it in the 2016 Atlantic Coast Conference (ACC) Championship game, but they really didn't see a lot of situations where they felt the statistics of running that play or the opposing defensive structure would give them a high probability of it being successful.

Fast forward to December 2019. Clemson was facing Ohio State in the Fiesta Bowl and the semifinal of the College Football Playoff (CFP) in Glendale, Arizona. Leading up to the game, Coach Elliott and his staff were looking at film of Ohio State, and in the process, Elliott noticed that in some situations,

Ohio State's defensive structure seemed vulnerable to the borrowed play he had put in his Play Book years earlier. They dug into the numbers and realized there was a high probability that the borrowed Virginia Tech play would work against Ohio State if the situation presented itself. As a result of this analysis, Coach Elliott added it to his Play Sheet that week.

Deep into the semifinal playoff game, the Clemson offense was down 23–21 in the fourth quarter. They were on Ohio State's thirty-four-yard line, and it was first down and ten. Up in the booth, Coach Elliott saw the formation of Ohio State's defense and glanced down at his Play Sheet. In his gut, he knew it was time to break the piggy bank. He quickly called in the play to the huddle. A few seconds later, Chris Fowler of ESPN announced, "Trevor Lawrence [the Clemson quarterback] thought run, dumps it over the middle, Etienne in space, Etienne to the ten...touchdown Tigers!"

That play put Clemson up 29–23 and ended up being the game-winning touchdown, sending Coach Elliott and Clemson to yet another College Football Playoff National Championship game.

Now let's break down what Coach Elliott did. He identified a play that fit his system and style. Then he added that play to his book of plays, and he evaluated scenarios each week to determine if that play would work based on the upcoming opponent and a matchup where this play was viable and applicable. He practiced the play with his team that week, and when the situation emerged in a critical moment, he glanced at his Play Sheet, recalled the play he'd learned about years prior, and executed it with success in a critical moment. This simple, repeatable process is performed by coaches across the country each week, and in this chapter I will teach you the high-level process of identifying and creating an inventory of plays, centralizing those plays into a Play Book, and organizing those plays so they are easily available when the time is right to use them to achieve more professional wins.

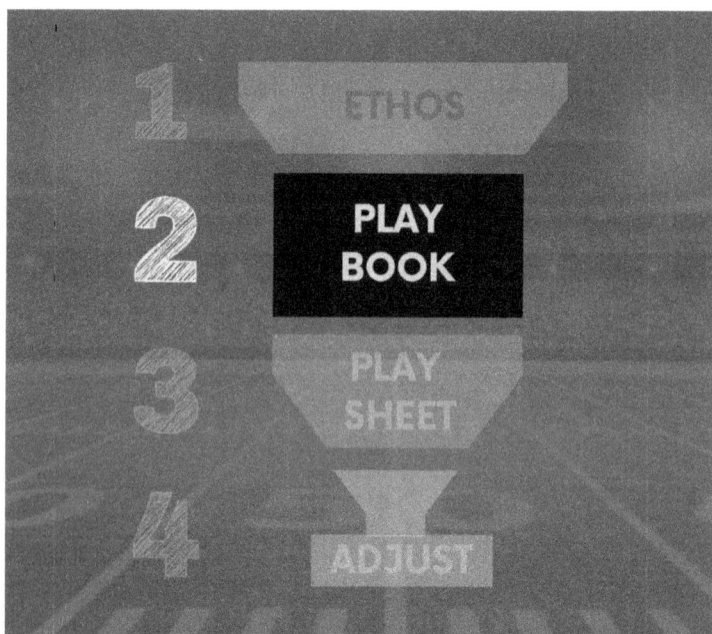

A PLAY BOOK IS THE HUB OF CONTINUOUS PROFESSIONAL DEVELOPMENT

The next step of this system is building a Play Book.

But what is a Play Book?

The football definition of a Play Book is a collection of all plays that a team can run during any game. A non-sports-related definition of a Play Book is a collection of usual tactics or methods.

In football circles, these are not one-off inventions and are quite common in their design and makeup. Today's Play Books are a compilation of way more than just plays. They are hundreds of pages long. Some coaches even have five-hundred-page Play Books if you were to print them out page by page. Play Books are a wiki for all things associated with that team and provide a consistent go-to source for all players, coaches, and staff. When someone joins the team, they receive a Play Book immediately, and it serves as an onboarding packet for that new team member.

Here is a list of things consolidated into an average football coach's Play Book:

- Team ethos, mission statements, and core values (usually at the start of the Play Book)
- Team goals and objectives
- Roles and responsibilities
- Team roster and directory
- Team policies and procedures
- Historical team statistics and records
- Team schedules (practice schedule, meeting schedule, etc.)
- Team rules
- Exercise programs
- Terminology/glossary
- The plays themselves with diagrams

Here is an old example of a page on procedures from the defensive section of a Play Book courtesy of Coach Dom Anderson, who is currently the defensive coordinator for Fayetteville State University.

PROCEDURES

Meetings

1. Be early!
2. Bring playbook, notebook, and writing utensil.
3. Sit straight, feet flat on the floor.
4. Listen, listen, *listen*.
5. Ask questions.
6. Take notes.

Practice

1. Be early!
2. Fight through soreness—you know whether you can practice or not!
3. Be enthusiastic.
4. Concentration.
5. Sprint on and off the field.
6. Sprint in and out of drills.
7. Listen to coaches' corrections of you and of other players.
8. If you are not in during a team period, stand together as a unit. That's so you can hear coaches' critiques as well as allowing coaches easy accessibility to you.
9. No discussion on the field. No debates. Coach is always right.
10. Every coach is your coach. We are a team.

11. Get better every time you take the field!!!
12. *Work—Compete—Have fun!!!*

Office

1. ▮▮▮▮▮ Football coaches have an open-door policy. You take priority over any meeting. See your coach if you have any problems, questions, or just want to talk.
2. Keep your coach informed on your academics.
3. Treat all support people with respect!

Game Weekend and Game Day

1. Be early to all team functions.
2. Sit together as a unit at all team functions.
3. Dress according to team codes.
4. Don't overeat!!! Drink plenty of fluids.
5. We huddle on Coach ▮▮▮▮▮ before we take the field.
6. When not on the field, sit or stand in assigned area depending on if you played in the series before. Everyone must be there to listen for corrections. Stay poised. We will get corrections or comments to you as soon as possible.
7. If ▮▮▮▮▮ State Defense is on the field and you are not in, have your helmet on and chinstrap buckled. You must be ready to go in at any time. Stand behind the Defensive Coaches.

8. Be enthusiastic, positive, and concentrate at all times. Stay in the game!
9. *Have fun!!!!!*
10. Play hard—never give up. Our offense can score points in a hurry.

Without this consolidated resource, coaches and players would spend precious time searching for information or items they needed to participate, improve, or execute their role on the team. Many coaches stressed that the Play Book contains the essential detailed information players and coaches need to translate strategy and game plans into effective tactics.

Journalist Richard Johnson wrote about all the artifacts a coach and their team use on game day to be successful. His article ended:

> For a player to be able to look at a coach signaling, or a diagram featuring Tupac and know his exact responsibility in a stadium with 80,000 people screaming on national television, it all got back to what's in the playbook. From the diagrams to the formation, to the team's ethos laid out across hundreds of pages, every bit of the playbook matters.[9]

---

9 Richard Johnson, "There's Tons of Other Stuff in Your Football Team's Playbook," Banner Society, August 15, 2019, https://www.bannersociety.com/2019/8/15/20726587/what-is-in-a-playbook-football.

It is critical to be thoughtful when considering what is in the Play Book. Unlike college football coaches, most business professionals have information stored in several places. Years ago when I did a personal inventory, I realized I had bookshelves full of books, hard drives with old Word documents, computers and browsers with saved desktop articles, pinned social media posts, a notebook full of quotes, and a Microsoft OneNote account full of a variety of key stats and reference guides. That is not an exhaustive list, and if someone asked me a question on a certain topic, I would scramble to find that piece of information across all these platforms or just speed-mumble part of the quote or stat I needed. I spent hours searching for information that I could have inventoried better. Having multiple sources of information made me feel disorganized, frustrated, and overwhelmed. It added to the overload.

The next steps to making you more effective in your day-to-day life are to inventory your sources of information, aggregate them into one place, and then organize them so you can quickly leverage or reference them when needed. Centralizing all your professional development ideas, concepts, quotes, plays, and so on into one place rather than multiple places eliminates another driver of information overload.

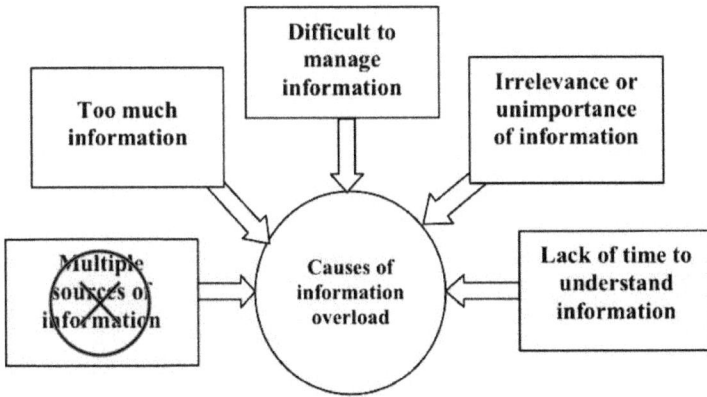

Diagram: Causes of information overload

1

DEFINE ETHOS

SELF ASSESS

SET OBJECTIVES

2

INVENTORY

CONSOLIDATE

ORGANIZE

3

PLAY

SHEET

4

ADJUST

ORGANIZING FOR SUCCESS: BUILD YOUR PLAY BOOK

Let's create your stock of tactics and methods. Hopefully, it will not be hundreds of pages long, but your ethos statement, OKRs, favorite quotes, favorite stats, key points from a book, and so on need to make their way into one source that can be stored and maintained long term.

The three steps to create your Play Book are:

1. **Inventory** your stock of concepts, ideas, and information.
2. **Consolidate** everything into one repository—your Play Book.

3. **Organize** your Play Book by creating a taxonomy of categories.

STEP 4: INVENTORY ALL YOUR SOURCES OF INFORMATION

If you're anything like me, rummaging through your hoarded content to decide what to include on one little sheet can feel impossible. Many people who I have taught this framework to had bookmarked articles on their browser, bookshelves full of books with highlighted sections or bookmarks, or note-taking applications full of one-liners, quotes, and ideas. Whatever your pile of data or sources looks like, jump in and start getting it organized so you can start the process of putting it in this one place, your Play Book. This exercise will take some time because, if you're like my wife, you'll find it a fantastic reason to donate books, delete files, and generally purge both actual and virtual desktops.

STEP 5: CONSOLIDATE YOUR STOCK OF PLAYS INTO ONE SOURCE—YOUR PLAY BOOK

Moving all your information from separate resources to a single place will be cumbersome at first, but it will pay dividends in the long term. Next time you ask yourself, *Where did I see that?* you'll be able to quickly reference your Play Book. Organizations and football teams leverage their Play Book as a vital tool for team communication and alignment. It helps users understand all the elements of the team so they can build and advance their knowledge.

Many practitioners of this approach search the web and app stores for a professional Play Book application or resource, but there are none out there that I recommend. Every coach, and many of the vendors for coaches, recommends keeping it simple. Many Play Books are PDFs, wiki sites, or football-specific software applications that are not adaptable to making a professional Play Book.

The simple approach that I recommend is to use an Excel spreadsheet, a single-user wiki application, Apple Notes, Microsoft OneNote, or any basic note-taking application that allows you to categorize your notes. There are many ways to do this, but try not to overcomplicate it. Simply get your information into one place.

STEP 6: ORGANIZE YOUR PLAY BOOK

For coaches, a critical function of success is finding the right plays to fit the system—just as professionals should focus on content and skills that highlight their strengths. Coaches organize types of plays and sections of their Play Book, and so should you.

Most coaches have running plays, passing plays, special team plays, goal line plays, after turnover plays, two-minute drill plays, blitz plays, and so on. An analogy I heard from coaches is that this part of the exercise is like cleaning and organizing your closet. When you buy new shoes, you add new shoes to the shoe section of your closet. So let's organize your professional plays.

Start by listing the areas that you're working on improving or strengthening in your day-to-day life or career, and make sure they align to your strengths and opportunities and also to your development OKRs. To get you thinking, here are some examples of the categories I, and others using this system, have used:

- Meetings
- Presentations
- Time management
- Strategic thinking
- Leadership
- Coaching and mentorship

Now you can either start pulling in all your concepts under each category, or you can just go source by source and tag their content to each category appropriately. The first time I did this I used the old sticky note approach and then translated it all to an Excel document that I still have today. As I matured my approach, I moved to a OneNote Play Book, as shown in the following image:

⟨   My Play Book   ⌕

Hurtak Ethos	Hosting a Meeting
Meetings	Running a Meeting
Presentations	Attending a Meeting
Mindfulness	Board Meetings
Listening	
Strategic Thinking	
Emotional Intelligence	
Time Management	
Leadership and Coaching	

Hosting a Meeting

- Clear objective (Have a Purpose in the Invite)
- Type of meeting in Subject (Brainstorm, Planning, Problem Solving)
- Assign roles (notes, leads) – share the workload
- How are you going to control the room?
- Assign action items and debrief if needed
- Mirroring / Conscious Communicator:
  - Be observant of other comm styles and personalities
  - (Relater, Socializer, Thinker, Director)

Here are a few **coaching** tips for this step:

- Add your ethos, core values, objectives, and roadmap to the front of this resource.
- Add a reference for each concept that allows you to link it to the source (book, article, etc.)
- Create or adopt a taxonomy of categories that will help you achieve your ethos and OKRs
- Map all the plays to each category. Note that some plays can span multiple categories.
- Build this resource in a way that makes sense to you. Personalize it, but make it simple and organized.
- Upload the resource to a secured cloud environment. I have met people who lost this document when a computer died or they left their company. That is a devastating experience, so be proactive about storing it in a place you can access securely from any device.
- Take your time the first time you do this. You have most likely spent years learning but have never aggregated or organized the information. The better the job you do now, the easier it will be to access and navigate all this content moving forward.

Congratulations! You have created your own personalized professional development Play Book. Your Play Book may not be exactly where you want it today, but over time this source will grow and become an invaluable resource for your continuous professional improvement. As you learn what works and what does not work over time, and as you identify innovative ideas, concepts, or skills, relentlessly update and organize your Play Book.

The most successful coaches evolve their Play Books as they gain more experience and continually iterate them as they learn what works or sometimes what does not work. Doing so will allow you to better align your strategy and objectives to your professional development tactics, helping you more effectively execute the professional plays or concepts you are working on to achieve your goals.

Going forward, a critical habit associated with your Play Book is continuously and relentlessly adding content to it as opposed to leaving information scattered across multiple sources. For example, the next time you're reading a book (which, hopefully, is aligned to your ethos and objectives) and you come across a paragraph or a quote that you feel would be helpful to adopt or apply, pull that information directly into your Play Book and add it to the appropriate category. In agile and lean practices, a continuous learning culture is a core competency of agility in a rapidly changing world. The process of continuous learning and creating new iterations of your Play Book should be ongoing.

SECOND-QUARTER HIGHLIGHTS

You created your own personalized professional development Play Book.

- You inventoried all your sources and your stock of ideas, concepts, quotes, best practices, and more in order to simplify your ability to access these items in the future.

- You consolidated everything from various sources and migrated them to one repository—your personal Play Book.

- Coaches organize types of plays and sections of their Play Book, and you organized your Play Book by creating a taxonomy of categories and mapped relevant plays to their respective categories. As a result, you will start to have a more focused resource and approach to help you improve current strengths and areas of opportunity.

- You learned about the concept of relentless and continuous improvement. As you learn what works and what does not work over time, and as you identify new ideas, concepts, or skills, you will continue to update, inventory, and archive your Play Book.

- You mitigated another key cause of cognitive load— multiple sources of information.

In summary, you developed a hub of personal development information for years to come, and you are now ready to move plays from your Play Book to your Play Sheet based on relevant and upcoming situations over the next few months, which will enable you to execute more effectively and achieve more professional wins.

PLAY BOOK TO PLAY SHEET

"A Play Sheet is an essential part of football. It ensures that everyone on the team is on the same page and knows exactly what they need to do in order to help their team win. Without it, chaos would ensue, and it would be very difficult for a team to be successful and achieve its goals of success."

—THOMAS CARRIERI, LOST IN BOSTON SPORTS

I am going to share two stories about professionals who have the same goal: execute effectively. One of them has good intentions to apply what they learned, and the other has a Play Sheet.

BUSINESS STORY: EVERYTHING BUT EXECUTION

A few years ago, I was mentoring a colleague named Jennifer. Jennifer had recently achieved a major career milestone and was promoted to management after years of being a solid individual contributor at her firm. She found herself overwhelmed as a new manager. She expressed the feeling that overnight, the number of meetings, emails, and fire drills multiplied by the number of direct reports on her new team. She found herself working all hours of the night and on weekends just to keep up. It was wearing on her, and she could feel herself and her team underperforming despite her giving every ounce of her energy to the new role. She quickly realized that operating the same way she had as an individual contributor would not generate results in her new role as a leader. Like many new leaders, she sought counsel on how to improve and find balance in her new role to overcome the sense that she was failing everyone.

Jennifer started seeking out information on how to improve from everywhere: Blinkist summaries, Google searches for how to manage your day-to-day, Audible book purchases galore, and a time management seminar called Organizing for Success.

After collecting all this advice, studying up on leadership and management, and attending the seminar, she felt much more confident that she was on her way to becoming a more productive leader in no time. While attending the seminar, Jennifer established a clear plan of what she needed to change and learned some great new ways to manage her day-to-day and team more effectively. The class ended around 4:00 p.m., and she was going to head home early, go to the gym, and decompress with some friends.

Then Jennifer got a flurry of texts. It was her team, her boss, and many others giving her news that something had gone wrong with their recent product launch. She immediately returned to the office, went to her desk, and dug into the problem. The team figured out the root cause and fixed the issue. When she looked at the clock, it was almost 11:30 p.m. She was exhausted.

The next day she went back into work around 7:00 a.m. and noticed that more than two hundred emails, which she'd received while she was away from the office, awaited her attention. She worked through them and continued reacting to whatever came her way that week. The weeks progressed, and her ability to find balance and drive quality through her team continued to suffer. No matter what she did, she felt she was letting people down: her boss, her team, her family, her friends, and herself.

The moral of the story is that she should have applied what she learned at that seminar rather than allowing those text messages to drive her back to square one.

Do you have a similar story?

A FOOTBALL STORY:
PLAY SHEET EXECUTION

In 2016, Coach Jake Spavital was the offensive coordinator and quarterback coach for the University of California, Berkeley.

On September 18, the Cal Bears (1-1) were hosting the eleventh-ranked Longhorns from the University of Texas (2-0). Coming into the game, Cal had not beaten a ranked team in almost four years. As Coach Spavital, his offensive coaches, and his offensive players studied their upcoming opponent, they decided on and prepared formations and plays specifically for when they went into the boundary, as they'd noticed a tendency of one of the Texas safeties.

Early in the game, Coach Spavital showed this formation, hoping it would work, but also to see how the Texas defense would adjust to it. After they ran the play, he noticed it played out just like he'd anticipated. Moments later, one of his wide receivers—Patrick Worstell, who was on the sideline and not even in the game—rushed over to Coach Spavital and said to him, "Coach, if you run that again with a double post into the middle of the field with a wheel route into the boundary, I can pull the safety with me and leave the wheel route wide open in the boundary."

Late into the first half, Coach Spavital and Cal found themselves trailing 31–21. Cal had the ball on the Texas 29 on second down and found themselves in the same situation they had prepared for and tested earlier in the game. Coach looked at his Play Sheet and immediately called the play where the wide receivers running the posts could pull the safety and create a lane for the receiver running the wheel route. He quickly called the play and made sure Patrick Worstell, the wide receiver who said he could pull the safety, entered the game.

Seconds later, the ESPN announcers yelled, "Webb (the Cal quarterback) goes downfield...and wide open. Room service. Touchdown Stovall!" The sideline erupted, and the entire offense rushed the wide receiver, Melquise Stovall, who'd scored. What the viewers or crowd did not know was that the play was a testimony that the team had prepared and studied their opponent and that they trusted each other and the coaches.

One of the ESPN announcers commented, "Stovall was wide open, Rob."

The other announcer replied, "Yeah, busted coverage, and they just ran a couple of in routes and then a little bit of a wheel to the outside, and there was total confusion on the backside for Texas. You got to go with the wheel and can't leave him alone."

When Coach Spavital was telling this story, he was energized. "The kids were so fired up after that play. That is my joy. When you see the kids come to you, and then it goes out there and works. That was a huge play at the time, and we ended up beating Texas, and that was a big deal. Everybody rushed the field at the end of that game, and you know, it was a really surreal moment...these were simple concepts, and we just had answers for what they were going to do." As Coach said, Cal won 50–43 and defeated a ranked team for the first time in almost four years. It was the first time they had ever beat Texas at home in their team's history. Practice and preparation can lead to performance or perfection, so let's help you score a win like Cal did back in 2016. (Apologies to my wife and in-laws, who are huge Longhorn fans.)

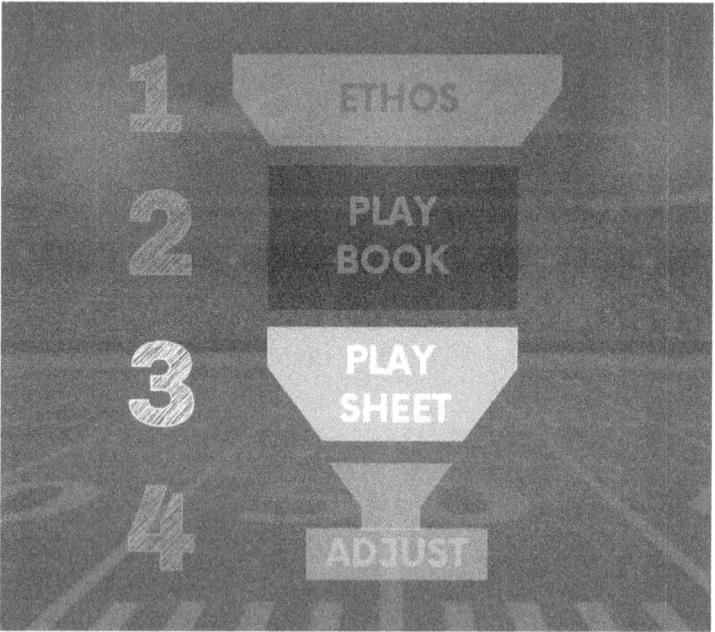

BUILD AND USE
YOUR PLAY SHEET

The only difference between Jennifer and Coach Spavital was their ability to follow their game plan and execute it in the moment. They both did all the research and homework to be better prepared for the scenario ahead of them, but Jennifer lacked a routine and a Play Sheet to remind her to execute what she had worked so hard to learn.

Most business professionals, like Jennifer, react to whatever fire drill or meeting invite comes their way each week. They often encounter critical decisions or crucial conversations and have to think quickly and make decisions, yet under this pressure, they lack confidence and effectiveness in their decision-making.

Now, if I asked where you would be on the third Tuesday in September at 2:00 p.m., it is likely you would have no clue. Ask that question to a football coach, however, and they can tell you.

All football coaches across the nation share a common bond. They are intentional. Each week they take the same simple, repeatable routines and processes and repeat them so they are as focused and prepared as possible for the next opponent and game. Which game plan they run and which plays they focus on are based on the situation that week, but the process of how they get from Saturday night to kickoff the next Saturday (Friday to Friday for high school) is like clockwork.

At the highest level, the following chart is an overview of what a calendar week looks like for an average coach, their staff, and their team (the examples we use are from the perspective of a college football coach, who typically plays their games on Saturdays).

SUNDAY	MONDAY	TUESDAY	WEDNESDAY	THURSDAY	FRIDAY	SATURDAY
GAME REVIEW	OVERALL GAME PLAN	PRACTICE (3RD DOWN)	PRACTICE (RED ZONE & GOAL LINE)	WALK THROUGH	PRACTICE	GAME DAY
FILM STUDY	PRACTICE	GAME PLAN	2-MINUTE DRILL	DRAFT SCRIPT & PLAY SHEET	FINALIZE SCRIPT & PLAY SHEET	WIN
SCOUTING REPORT	GAMEPLAN (3RD DOWN)		WALK THROUGH			
OPPONENT TENDENCY CHART						

Regardless of your football IQ, the takeaway of Sunday to Saturday here is a funnel. Coaches scout the upcoming opponent, evaluate the opponent's strengths and weaknesses, and cross-reference that with their own team's ability to match up. From this information they establish a game plan. Then they filter out plays from their Play Book that are relevant to that week's approach or focus. They test these in practice and iterate until they build their Play Sheet for the week. Over time these routines become repeatable week over week and enable the coaching staff to help improve the team's abilities and performance over the course of the season.

What the coaches I spoke to did not know, but was another epiphany to me, is that they follow a widely known formula in industrial engineering, IT, manufacturing, or any industry that evaluates quality and improvement. It is known as the Shewhart cycle, the control cycle, or the PDCA cycle—the most popular of the three names today is PDCA, which stands for Plan, Do, Check, Act. This is simply an iterative design method for continuous improvement.

- **Plan**: Establish objectives and routines to deliver required results.
- **Do**: Carry out the objectives.
- **Check**: Evaluate the results in terms of performance.
- **Act (or Adjust)**: Maintain the change or begin the cycle again to further improve.

Let's relate the PDCA cycle to a typical week of a football coach.

- **Plan**: The coach builds a game plan each week by conducting repeatable routines.
- **Do**: The coach practices the game plan and proposed plays from Monday to Friday.
- **Check**: Over the course of the week, the coach and their players check to see which plays work and which plays will not make the cut.
- **Act (or Adjust)**: From a week of evaluation and preparation, the coach adjusts their play script and Play Sheet for the game on Saturday and runs (acts out) those plays in the game.

In this chapter, we will take a glimpse into the brilliance and simplicity of how football coaches prepare each week, move from Play Book to Play Sheet, and establish simple, repeatable routines. Simultaneously, we will demonstrate how they follow the PDCA cycle and, in turn, leverage this methodology to help you build and use your own personalized Play Sheet.

- Step 7: Build your Game Plan (Plan)
- Step 8: Build your Play Sheet (Plan)
- Step 9: Use your Play Sheet (Do) and Evaluate your play performance (Check)

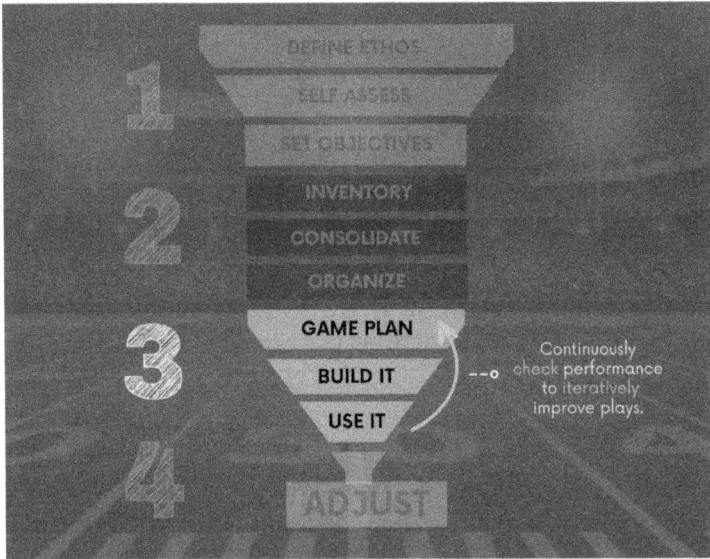

Please note that we will discuss Act (or Adjust) in the Fourth-Quarter chapter and focus only on Plan, Do, and Check in this chapter.

STEP 7: BUILD YOUR GAME PLAN

"By failing to prepare, you are preparing to fail."

—BEN FRANKLIN

In the continuous improvement model, the first phase is Plan. The Plan phase consists of detecting an opportunity and planning for the change. Therefore, ask yourself, *What areas of development are most important for me to focus on?*

To answer this question, remember to reflect back on your Play Book mission, strategy, and OKRs. Study them for a few minutes, and keep them in mind as you start this exercise. You will use them as a filter to choose where to start. Now think about the next thirty to ninety days. What objectives and key results do you want to accomplish over the next few months? Are there any critical skills you need to enhance based on recent feedback? Are you preparing for something that would be more successful if you sharpened certain skills needed to execute more effectively in that moment? These questions can determine whether you have a calculated game plan over the next few months.

Although the context may differ, coaches go through a similar exercise to establish a game plan each week once one game ends and a new week of preparation begins. In the figure that demonstrated how coaches prepare each week, Sunday's preparation enabled the staff to create a game plan before practice on Monday. The four areas of focus on Sunday were a game review of their own previous game, a film study on their upcoming opponent, a scouting report, and a tendency chart. With these pieces of information, coaches can quickly collaborate on a game plan they wish to install that week and teach in practice. Let's quickly dig into these items to understand how they relate to your Play Sheet.

- **Game Review:** Coaches perform a retrospective of their team's last game using game film to determine the good, the bad, and the ugly of how the team and players performed so they can reinforce strengths and coach to opportunities week over week. This helps them get crisp on what they need to improve on in the following week and clarifies where they should focus their coaching time with players.

- **Film Study on the Opponent**: Coaches scout the opponent by breaking down three to four games' worth of film of their opponent in order to formulate a scouting report and game plan. Watching the film of the opponent requires more of the coaches' time than watching their own team since it is less familiar to them. In the professional world, you could equate this to competitive intelligence.

  The objective here is to answer questions like the following:
  - What plays do they like to run?
  - What formations or how do they like to run those plays?
  - When do they like to run those plays?
  - What matchups can we make to exploit their weaknesses or prepare for their strengths?

- **Scouting Report and Opponent Tendency Chart**: Teams develop scouting reports to help them better understand the strengths and weaknesses of the opposing team and some of the players on that team. The report includes injury updates, key statistics, information on what their own team would do well against this player or system, and a projection of what their team should do against this player or overall team. Complementary to the scouting report is the tendency stat sheet we discussed in Chapter 1. This is a summary of opposing team stats at a glance that allows coaches to see what type of call the opposing team makes most often, organized by down and distance, personnel, formation, and so on.

With this analysis and the associated insights, coaches are ready to formulate a plan of attack, also known as a game plan. In 2017, *USA Today* contributor Ralph Russo wrote about how a college football coach plans for the game. He stated that "putting together a game plan is an elaborate exercise in the art—and science—of analyzing an opponent's tendencies and patterns and determining how best to exploit them. It's mixing and matching. What do we like to do and when? What do they like to do and when? Throw out the stuff that won't work, keep what should, and then figure out what are (hopefully) the best plays to run in the upcoming game."[10]

---

10   Ralph D. Russo, "Plan of Attack: How a College Football Coach Game-Plans," *USA Today*, August 17, 2017, https://www.usatoday.com/story/sports/ncaaf/2017/08/17/plan-of-attack-how-a-college-football-coach-game-plans/104676406.

Over the last few chapters, you have done the analysis, homework, and preparation. Now it is time to build your game plan so you can quickly build out your Play Sheet. To build your game plan for the next thirty to ninety days, you will review and reference the following items:

- Your ethos
- Your prioritized strengths and opportunities
- Your objectives and key results
- Your calendar of professional events over the next ninety days
- Any 360 feedback, coaching, or performance evaluations you received

Now, with those artifacts or references in hand, determine your areas of focus for the next month or quarter. This will help you filter from Play Book to Play Sheet. Ask yourself which three to five most important or relevant categories from your Play Book you should funnel down to your Play Sheet. Consider these your base categories of plays.

The hardest part of this exercise is narrowing your Play Sheet down to these categories versus trying to tackle everything you want to improve on in your professional development. In a simple spreadsheet, start creating columns for each of the play categories that you chose from your Play Book. Once you have an idea of the areas from your Play Book you would like to focus on, you are ready for the next step, building your Play Sheet.

STEP 8: BUILD YOUR PLAY SHEET

The next step of this system is the one you have been waiting for. We are ready to build your Play Sheet. This artifact is the last part of the Plan phase of the continuous improvement cycle, and once developed, it will enable you to execute and implement the changes you desire. But what exactly is a Play Sheet?

In football, a Play Sheet is a list of plays used by the coach to call plays from. Play Sheets come in all shapes and sizes. Some are small, and some are the equivalent to a menu at the Cheesecake Factory. In my research and discussions, no two were exactly alike, and this is another reason I think they have application to the business world. They can be personalized to fit your style. Most coaches inherited their first Play Sheet but, over time, customized it to their systems, style, comfort, and needs. Many coaches said you have to find what works for you when creating or customizing your Play Sheet (and the same will be true for you). For real examples of coaching Play Sheets or Play Sheet templates, go to our website *www. myplaysheet.com*.

These examples are organized by sets or categories of plays. All the categories may not be the same, but based on the system, opponent, or coach, that Play Sheet is organized so it can be

1st | 2nd Down

21 Personnel

#	
1	
2	
3	
4	

12 Personnel

#	
5	
6	
7	
8	
9	

10 Personnel

#	
1	
2	
3	
4	

11 Personnel

#	
1	
2	
3	
4	

3rd Long (10+)

11 Personnel

#	
1	
2	
3	
4	

10 Personnel

#	
1	
2	
3	

3rd Medium (6-9)

11 Personnel

#	
1	
2	
3	
4	
5	

3rd Short (3-5)

11 Personnel

#	
1	
2	
3	

Back Half (-30 to -15)

21 Personnel

#	
1	
2	
3	

12 Personnel

#	
1	

10 Personnel

#	
1	
2	

11 Personnel

#	
1	
2	

Red Zone (-15 to Goal Line)

21 Personnel

#	
1	
2	

12 Personnel

#	
1	

11 Personnel

#	
1	

Time-Out Chart

Time Outs-Us			
1st Half	1	2	3
2nd Half	1	2	3

Time Outs-Opponents			
1st Half	1	2	3
2nd Half	1	2	3

Game/Impact Plays Notes

Personnel Notes

referenced and used at a glance when the play clock is ticking. Here are some example sections you may see on a Play Sheet:

- Script section—first few plays of a half
- Situation section
  - 2nd and short
  - 2nd and long
  - 3rd and short
  - 3rd and long
  - Red zone
  - Goal line
  - Big play
  - Less than two minutes
- Personnel or players section—used when you want to match up certain players
- Key stats and tips section—including referee names
- Timeout section—used to track how many timeouts remain

Here are the high-level steps to building your first Play Sheet. In this section, we will explain each part in more detail.

1. Pick three to five categories aligned to your game plan to focus on for the next thirty to ninety days.
2. Map three to five plays from your Play Book to each category.

3. Create a key stats or tendencies section.
4. Laminate or digitize your Play Sheet.

Pick Three to Five Categories Aligned to Your Game Plan to Focus on for the Next Thirty to Ninety Days

I recommend keeping the first iteration of your Play Sheet simple and not overloading it with too many categories. As you get more proficient and comfortable with this exercise, you can expand the scope of your Play Sheet and add more categories, but for now simply reference your game plan and pick three to five categories that you are working to improve over the next thirty to ninety days.

These categories should be the same categories you have in your Play Book. But instead of trying to run your entire Play Book, we're going to pick the top plays aligned to your game plan.

For example, let's say a football coach has one hundred plays in his Play Book. He will not use all one hundred plays each week. After evaluating the other team's strengths and weaknesses, he may immediately cut those one hundred plays down to sixty in an effort to filter what plays will work for the week ahead. Then, from those sixty plays, he may identify a subset of his strongest plays. At this point he starts to identify the key plays to run in specific situations against the opponent at hand.

You will do the same here. The following were some of the category examples from a Play Book I shared. For this exercise,

I will use the persona of a new manager working on being a better leader than doer. As a result, that new manager looks at her OKRs and picks the following five areas to focus on for the weeks and months ahead rather than trying to improve all the areas in her Play Book.

PLAY BOOK CATEGORY	
ORGANIZE MEETINGS	✓
CONDUCT MEETINGS	
LISTENING	
STRATEGIC THINKING	✓
DELEGATION SKILLS	✓
EMOTIONAL INTELLIGENCE	✓
TIME MANAGEMENT	✓
PRESENTATIONS	

- Category 1: Organizing meetings
- Category 2: Strategic thinking
- Category 3: Delegation skills
- Category 4: Emotional Intelligence
- Category 5: Time management

Map Your Top Three to Five Plays per Category

Now, using your Play Book, go to the category of plays you have in the first column of your Play Sheet. Review all the hacks, quotes, and so on in that category, and pick the three to five things that are most impactful to making that skill stronger. Then add them to the rows in the first column of your Play Sheet.

The hard part here will be summarizing what you want to remember in a succinct way. You don't need to include the entire paragraph from the book you referenced; simply write five to seven words that summarize the key points and will jog your memory when you have just a few seconds to glance at the play prior to trying to deploy that category of plays. This document is simply a guide to remembering what you already know in the moments that matter most.

For reference, here is an example of a group of plays for Category 5: Time management.

TIME MANAGEMENT
PLAY 1: COVEY: "SCHEDULE YOUR PRIORITIES DON'T PRIORITIZE YOUR SCHEDULE"
PLAY 2: DO YOUR MOST MEANINGFUL WORK FIRST
PLAY 3: ALLEN: "YOU CAN DO ANYTHING, BUT NOT EVERYTHING"
PLAY 4: SCHEDULE 30 MINUTES ON SUNDAY TO PLAN YOUR CALENDAR EACH WEEK
PLAY 5: FRANKLIN: PICK 3 THINGS EACH DAY YOU WISH TO ACCOMPLISH AND FOCUS ON THOSE FIRST. FILTER OUT THE REST.

Now simply repeat this step for each column (or category) until you have three to five plays per category. For examples of personalized Play Sheets go to our website *www.myplay sheet.com*. You will see the examples are not high-tech or fancy. They are simply an at-a-glance cheat sheet to remind me of what I already knew but did not want to forget under pressure.

Create a Key Stats or Notes Section

Most coaches carve out a space on their Play Sheet for key stats, reminders, and tips. These may say, "Watch the safety on third and short," "Number 45 blitzes when his hand is on the turf," or "Eighty-five percent of the time they blitz on third and two." These are just at-a-glance stats that are important enough for the coach to put them in front of his eyes when dealing with critical situations during the game. Some coaches even put the names of the referees on there so they don't forget them when they want to politely challenge a call on the field.

Have you ever created a script for a big presentation and written a few words in large print, circled them, or underlined them to remind yourself to do that one thing in the presentation? I always jot down notes like "Breathe," "Slow down," or "Read the room." Others may place sticky notes on the lectern or on their computer screen if they're in a virtual meeting. This is simply a way to remind yourself in a critical moment how to overcome your opportunities or play to your strengths. Coaches do the same thing on their Play Sheet, and I recommend you do the same on yours.

In business we often have certain numbers that are key to our world. So feel free to place some of these in this section so you always have them at hand. Some professionals like to put their scorecard metrics and actuals here. This section serves as their mini scoreboard, reminding them of the objectives they are trying to achieve in their role.

Many people like to put reminders for presentations here. For example, the person or audience you're presenting to may require you to focus specifically on one thing, so put those tips in that section as well. One sales rep I know used to include the city he was in so he didn't accidentally mix up cities when he was traveling from location to location. Just like coaches do for referees, many put names of key people in the meeting or reminders about these people, like their children's names or hobbies, to help remind them of personal details that will help build their relationships with those people.

This is the most fluid section of your Play Sheet, and you have liberty to swap things in and out of it as frequently as necessary. Personally, I laminate my Play Sheet and keep this space blank so that I can use a washable marker to put things on it every morning or every week.

Laminate or Digitize Your Play Sheet

Once it is filled out, you can use your Play Sheet in a variety of ways, but making it look like the one a coach uses during a game is a fun exercise.

Laminate It

I recommend laminating it, but if you don't have easy access to a laminating machine, you can use clear or transparent folders, which provides the same look and function as a laminated sheet. This may seem lame, but I promise you it'll feel legit. The reason for doing this is that you may want to mark up your Play Sheet, and you can use the laminated sheet or the clear folder to mark some things down without making permanent changes. You can circle or star a play that matters most for you to have that day and then change the starred play the next day when you're working on another skill.

Digitize It

During the pandemic, many people, including me, were on Zoom, Teams, or Skype meetings all day every day. Many of us upgraded our home office with standing desks and multiple screens. As a result, many of us who use a Play Sheet started using their second screen as a place to always have our Play Sheet visible in a way that no one could see we were using it. Make it a PDF, a PowerPoint slide, your home screen, or whatever you like; creating a go-to digital copy of your Play

Sheet is more functional than ever before in our new hybrid or remote office environment. I experimented with making it the lock screen and home screen on my phone at times to remind myself to constantly reference it so I could implement the skills I was working on improving.

However you choose to design it, the most important rule here is to *always have it on hand.*

Film Study: Coach Lincoln Riley's Approach to Cutting Plays for the Play Sheet

When attending the Texas High School Coaches Association Conference in 2021, I listened to former Oklahoma Sooners coach (now with the University of Southern California—USC) and Texas native Lincoln Riley speak about his routine. On Tuesday mornings his staff and players practiced scripted third-down scenarios. He told a story about a week during which they practiced about eighteen third-down plays to whittle down which third and short and third and long plays would make it onto the Play Sheet.

Coach Riley was relentless in his approach to cutting plays throughout the week to keep things simple on game day. He always narrows down to no more than twenty-eight plays on a Play Sheet. Not twenty-nine. In his speech, he said he wanted to eliminate as many variables as possible. "I believe that 80 percent of the script needs to be ready against anything they do, and if so, our team will be good. If we get any higher than

80 percent, then they are not going to be in an advantageous position. The other 20 percent should be specific to the opponent, but no more than that because if more than 20 percent, then we are getting away from the strengths of the team."[11]

He also reinforced the risk of introducing too many new things each week. He and his staff highlight plays on their list to differentiate new plays from existing plays. If they see too much highlighted on the sheet, they need to reevaluate the plan because they know this amount of new information will cause too much complexity and—you guessed it—cognitive load for the players to absorb come game day.

Coach Riley further addressed the concept of filtering or cutting plays. He said that coaches and others had asked him if they could have more than twenty-eight plays, and he said no. The tough calls during the week to get to twenty-eight help us to be better prepared for the game. He said, "If you are not going to call it or if you waver at all about the play, cut it. It's just not right for this week's big moments."

Consistently filtering out what makes the twenty-eight-play cut simplifies the process and simplifies the amount of information players need to master each week. This helps each player avoid confusion and feel confident about the game plan.

---

11 Lincoln Riley, speech at Texas High School Coaches Association Convention, San Antonio, Texas, July 18–21, 2021.

The transfer of your plays from Play Book to Play Sheet can further decrease the cognitive load in day-to-day situations. Let's summarize the causes of information overload that we just reduced in the creation of your professional Play Sheet:

- You centralized all your plays in your Play Sheet to eliminate multiple sources of information.

- You chose the key sets of plays aligned to your mission and OKRs to put on your Play Sheet. As Coach Riley did, you simplified your game plan and reduced the possibility of having too much information or irrelevant information when it is time to execute.

- You organized your three to five plays in each category and personalized the design or organization of your professional Play Sheet, making your go-to plays easier to recall and apply in the moment, therefore making it easier to manage the information now and in the future.

- Lastly, you overcame the challenge of not having enough time to understand the information because you have already done all the preplanning and preparation for your Play Book and now your Play Sheet. Having your personalized Play Sheet on hand will enable you to quickly recall what plays you are working on and jog your memory of the concepts you learned previously.

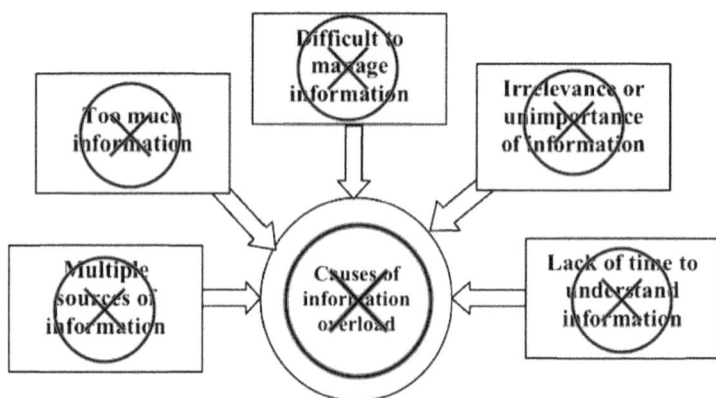

Diagram: Causes of information overload

STEP 9: USE YOUR PLAY SHEET AND CHECK ITS EFFECTIVENESS

Congratulations on building your personalized Play Sheet! It is important to take some time to celebrate this win. Too often we are hard on ourselves, but if you have gotten this far in the process, you are working hard and deserve to celebrate your progress to date.

Next, you need to implement the skills in your daily actions, so I will teach you how to use this tool as part of your daily routine. Implementing these changes or improvements is part of the Do phase of the continuous improvement cycle.

The constant use, review, and updating of this simple resource is imperative. If you don't use it, you are like a player or team not practicing but expecting to execute effectively in the game. Over time you will forget to use your Play Sheet and will not mature the skills aligned to your objectives. Using your Play Sheet needs to become a simple, repeatable routine in your life so that you can turn the concepts in your Play Book and Play Sheet into autonomous skills in your life.

The common theme among all the coaches I interviewed is the repeatable process they go through each week that leads to building a Play Sheet for the game ahead.

Before we dive into some tips on how to integrate the Play Sheet into your daily routine, it may be helpful to share why the application of these plays over and over has influenced your development.

Practice Makes Perfect:
Create Weekly Routines to Use Your Play Sheet

As you start using your Play Sheet, it will feel weird and unnatural, and people may wonder what you keep referencing. Despite its cultural adoption in the football world, it is not a cultural norm in the professional world or any context outside of calling football plays. You will have to overcome your discomfort and trust the process, but in order to get comfortable, you will need to practice using your Play Sheet over and over until it is part of your daily routine.

The first time you run your plays, they won't immediately be successful. Many of the coordinators we interviewed spent a lot of their week looking for their opponent's tendencies. They did this because they could anticipate opportunities in the moment.

Many of the offensive coordinators spent hours each week looking through film to identify vulnerabilities in their opponent's defense. Once they found these tendencies or vulnerabilities, coaches would then identify what plays had worked for other teams against this opponent and what plays they had in their Play Book that would expose these opportunities. They would focus on mastering those plays with their players throughout the week, knowing that if they executed them, they would have a good chance of working and giving them a better opportunity to win that play, that series, and the game.

But just knowing the best play to run does not mean it will work every single time. There are a lot of variables in a game, and sometimes luck is a factor. Just because the play didn't work the first or second time a team tried it doesn't mean they gave up on their game plan.

It is important that you trust the process and keep running your plays where you identify them to be advantageous to your professional development and to achieve more professional wins even if the plays don't work the first, second, or tenth time.

You must practice implementing these concepts repeatedly. With more reps, you will become more precise and effective at running each play.

In the 99U book *Maximize Your Potential*, bestselling author Joshua Foer is asked what the stages of skill acquisition are. In his answer he refers to three stages that psychologists identified in the 1960s:

- Stage 1: Cognitive Phase
    - Foer says, "We start in the 'cognitive phase' during which we're intellectualizing the task, discovering new strategies, to perform better, and making lots of mistakes...we are consciously focusing on what we are doing."[12]
    - Coaches leverage their film study and game plan to develop new approaches, perform better week over week, and coach the players.
    - When you build your game plan and intentionally start identifying which plays to run and when, you will immediately be in this phase. You will find places where the plays work and where they do not; you will make mistakes and will see some

---

12 Joshua Foer, "Learning to Live Outside Your Comfort Zone," in Maximize *Your Potential: Grow Your Expertise, Take Bold Risks, & Build an Incredible Career*, ed. Jocelyn K. Glei (Las Vegas, NV: Amazon Publishing, 2013), 96.

success, and over time you will start to perform the plays more effectively.

- Stage 2: Associative Phase
  - According to Foer, the second phase is "when we're making fewer errors, and gradually getting better."[13]
  - This is exactly what coaches said about running their plays as the season progressed. The more they practiced, executed, analyzed how they performed, and practiced again, the better they performed each play. This did not happen overnight. It took practice, and over time they executed each play with fewer errors.
  - When you use your Play Sheet week in and week out, you will make some mistakes but will gradually start to execute your plays more effectively. You will determine when and where they are most effective. You will determine which plays need more reps than others. And you will get a feel for which plays match your style and which plays may not be suited for you overall.

---

13   Foer, "Learning to Live Outside Your Comfort Zone," 96.

- Stage 3: Autonomous Phase
  - "Finally, we arrive at the 'autonomous stage' when we turn on autopilot and move the skill to the back of our proverbial mental filing cabinet and stop paying conscious attention to it," says Foer.[14]
  - Over the course of a season, certain plays are "go-to" or base plays for a team regardless of the opponent at hand. They don't start the season that way, but over time they become the plays you rely on when it matters most.
  - When your plays reach this stage, you can start to remove them from your Play Sheet and move on to the next skills you wish to develop and master. Once these plays become habits, you will see the return on your investment of time and arduous work. You will further grow and develop. And you will be able to free up your Play Sheet for some new plays so you can develop more good habits.

As you start using your Play Sheet, I suggest you create and practice two routines—pregame and in-game—to help build confidence in using your Play Sheet. The objective of this step is to make the use of your Play Sheet autonomous so that you can continuously improve and master the skills on it.

---

14 Foer, "Learning to Live Outside Your Comfort Zone," 96.

Create Your Pregame Routine:

Use Your Play Sheet to Plan for the Day or Week Ahead

It is Sunday evening, and Felix, a manager at a marketing firm who recently built his personal Play Sheet, is getting ready for a big Monday. As usual for a Sunday night, he scans his Outlook calendar and recognizes some important meetings and conversations coming up. What is different this time is that he also has his personalized Play Sheet in front of him, and he begins to cross-reference his Play Sheet with his Outlook calendar.

In his mind, Felix envisions himself on the sideline of his day with his laminated sheet of paper, staring at several business-day situations. He has done all the preparation he needs to be ready for this important Monday, and now he just needs to have confidence in himself and his ability to call plays.

He sees the first meeting of his day on his calendar. It is an 8:00 morning huddle with his direct reports. He reflects on his objective, the intended outcome of that meeting, and how he can be most effective in it. Glancing down at his Play Sheet, Felix sees two plays he is currently working to improve as a manager and leader of people. He sees the play "listening more" and the play "letting my leaders lead." As a result, his memory is jogged; he will do just that and go into the meeting with a plan on how he can be more successful so the meeting can be effective.

Next he sees a one-on-one meeting with his boss later that Monday morning, from 10:00 to 10:30. In his last one-on-one, he received coaching from his boss on being more succinct in his updates to senior leadership. With that development objective in mind, he again glances at his Play Sheet, at the effective communication set of plays, and sees the quote "verbatim retention." His executive coach shared this concept with him recently to help him improve his ability to deliver succinct, clear communication to an executive audience. Verbatim retention means delivering a message in such a way that if you saw a person from the audience in the hallway three weeks later, they could repeat your main points from the meeting back to you verbatim.

With that quick reminder from his Play Sheet, Felix feels he will be more intentional in what he says or doesn't say to his leader and how he says it in their one-on-one. He remembers to speak more slowly, use fewer words, repeat the main points, and ask his boss if he needs any clarification at the end. He also quickly jots some notes in his Outlook calendar to remind himself of the key points his leader needs to know. With this routine and resource, Felix will now have this information at his fingertips when 10:00 a.m. rolls around in case he is rushing from meeting to meeting.

Late on this important Monday, Felix sees a block on his calendar from 3:30 p.m. to 4:00 p.m. that simply says to "recognize the team." Lately he and his team have been so busy that he feels they do not spend enough time giving meaningful recognition to one another. He glances at his Play Sheet;

under the leadership set of plays, it says "recognition but no weak claps." Have you ever been in a meeting where someone is thanked or recognized, and everybody gives a round of applause, but the applause is quite pitiful and feels almost insincere? People barely even connect one palm to their other, and they may not even clap more than once. That is a weak clap, and I would bet that the person being recognized didn't fill up with pride and appreciation as the person recognizing them intended.

If you are going to thank someone or recognize them, make it count. "Don't give a weak clap" is something Felix read in a recent LinkedIn article, and he wants to make this recognition count today. With both his Play Sheet and his calendar, he feels more equipped to execute more intentionally and effectively in his recognition moments later that day.

What Felix just did was what most football coaches do prior to each game. They draft up a script for the first few plays to start a game or for the first half, or for if they see a certain formation that is aligned to their research on tendencies. On Sunday night, Felix created a blueprint of which plays he would run the next day, and as a result, he felt prepared and more mindful about his approach to a packed Monday.

Like Felix, let's take a few moments to cross-reference your calendar with your Play Sheet. This is like doing a walkthrough in a football practice.

1. Identify a time each day or week when you can slow down to speed up and carve out ten minutes to repeat this routine. Block off that time as a no-fly zone or untouchable time. Mark it private; mark it in red—do whatever you need to do to let yourself and anyone else know that this time is *not to be scheduled over*. People who are most effective with this approach carve out time each day as part of their routine to prepare for the day, week, or situation ahead.

2. Pull up your Outlook, work, or personal calendar, and identify a day in the next week or two when you have a series of important interactions or meetings.

3. Pull up your Play Sheet.

4. Looking at your calendar, ask yourself what key meetings you have, and create some what-if scenarios. What do you need to do so that they will be as successful as possible for you and the other participants?

5. Now ask yourself what types of plays on your Play Sheet match your answers to Step 4.

6. Envision one of these meetings, and in your mind, simulate the scenario and visualize yourself using

a particular play in that moment. Ask yourself, *Will this work here?* If yes, map that play to that meeting, mentally or on your calendar.

7. Do this for each meeting that day or even that week.

This preparation will help you prior to your game day. In the coming sections of this chapter and the next chapter, we will discuss how to use your Play Sheet on the day of the scenario, how to reflect on how it worked, and other effective ways to maximize the use of your new tool.

Create Your In-Game Routines: Use the Play Sheet in Real Time

Slowing down to speed up will make you a more effective play caller, but there will be times when you will want to reference your Play Sheet in the moment in high-pressure situations. Here is how to leverage your Play Sheet in real time, just like the coaches you met earlier.

First, you *must* always have your Play Sheet on hand. If you are working virtually, I recommend having it printed out in front of you or on your second screen at all times. If you are in a physical environment, then you may want to have it on your phone or in your hands in every meeting. No one will notice it is there.

Imagine you are walking to your next meeting, which you know is a critical sales meeting with a buyer to help you get a big project for your firm. You have been working on improving your ability to influence. You've recently read books on influencing others. You glance at your sales and influence section and see a few plays like "get them to say yes" (Zig Ziglar), "smile" (Dale Carnegie), and "use liking as a persuasion weapon" (Robert Cialdini). You look over these plays right before you walk into the room. Once you enter, you walk over to the decision-maker, greet and compliment them, smile, and ask them questions that you know will be answered with a yes. You are intentional in every action. The meeting is about to begin, and you quickly glance at your Play Sheet's effective communication section. You see the plays "be concise," "engage your audience," and "summarize your key points." The clock is ticking. The huddle breaks, and you are ready to run your play.

In the previous exercise, you prepared ahead of time for meetings, but in this exercise, I want you to pick a meeting in the coming week and practice using your Play Sheet within a limited amount of time or under pressure. Sometimes a coach goes in with a plan but must leverage certain plays from their Play Sheet that are not on their script of plays for that game because the situation is not playing out exactly as they'd hoped or expected. The coach is still prepared for this adjustment, and their Play Sheet acts as a calming mechanism to quickly allow them to reference some other plays so they can still be competitive that day.

Technically, in this exercise, we don't want you to plan ahead, but you need to practice using the Play Sheet spontaneously and in two ways:

1. Prior to walking into or virtually joining a meeting with your Play Sheet in hand, review your Play Sheet and practice quickly trying to apply a play in the meeting that is starting in just a few minutes.

2. Have your Play Sheet in the meeting, and when an unexpected situation arises, be present, and be mindful. Reference your Play Sheet, and run a play in the moment.

These are different applications of your tool, but just as important. Practice makes perfect. Just like coaches and players during the week of practice or in a game, you will start to create a neurological feedback loop. Cues like attending a meeting, having a one-on-one, or planning for your week will naturally become associated with using your Play Sheet to remind you of the play you want to run in that situation, and your reward will be more professional wins.

Coaching Tips for Using Your Play Sheet

- **Outsmart yourself by setting reminders**. One best practice is to leverage your phone, watch, Alexa, or calendar notifications to remind you to run certain plays at certain times. Set an alarm (on silent, of course) right before you go into the meeting or during the meeting to nudge you to remember a key stat you want to reinforce or an approach you want to take in the meeting.

- **Minimize your risk early in your skill development by practicing in safe nonwork environments.** A clever way to get more practice reps without taking on the highest risk to your job or situation is to practice in safe nonwork environments. For example, I sit on some nonprofit boards, and I've often tried out my concepts when leading those teams before trying to apply them to situations in my career. I get to practice them and improve on them, and when I feel more confident in using them, I start applying them in those more critical situations.

Evaluate Play Performance (Check)

In project and portfolio management, many organizations practice some sort of agile methodology. At the core of this methodology is the Agile Manifesto. This collection of twelve principles of agile dates back in the 1990s, when software developers gathered to determine a better, more responsive way to deliver work. The Agile Manifesto emphasizes the importance of continuous improvement through the following principle: "At regular intervals, the team reflects on how to become more effective, then tunes and adjusts its behavior accordingly."[15]

A major part of the continuous improvement cycle is measuring or analyzing performance against the target, or the Check phase of PDCA.

For both scenarios where you used your Play Sheet spontaneously, carve out time after the meeting and reflect on how well you picked the play and executed the skill you are improving. Think about and take notes on where this play is relevant to other meetings or situations, and when you prepare for the next day or week, think about running that play in that scenario again.

As discussed, coaches dedicate time to performing a retrospective on how their team executed during the game. They delegate film study to different coaches to review what the team did well and did not do so well. They also devour hours of film on their opponent to determine their tendencies, weaknesses, skill gaps, and so on. Watching film on their own team helps them find where players missed tackles, made unforced errors, made turnovers, loafed versus hustled, missed assignments, and much more. All this analysis on the prior performance is simply a check on where they can reinforce strengths or coach

---

15   Kent Beck et. al., "Principles Behind the Agile Manifesto," accessed February 13, 2024, https://agilemanifesto.org/iso/en/principles.html.

on opportunities to improve week over week. During each week, they also relentlessly practice their plays and further evaluate what is working and what needs continuous improvement. They even simulate scenarios and walk through them with the team during practice. You can do the same in your pre-game routines. Imagine yourself in the moment, running the play again, and consider how you would do it differently this time around to improve your performance or execution.

Many coaches I interviewed said they coached harder after a win than they did after a loss because their team tends to get overconfident or complacent. You must keep improving week after week; otherwise, you may win a game here or there, but you will not achieve your ultimate goal.

The Check process is not necessarily a sequential step but a continuous exercise that you should perform to turn plays from good to great or autonomous in nature. (See the arrow to the right of "Use it.")

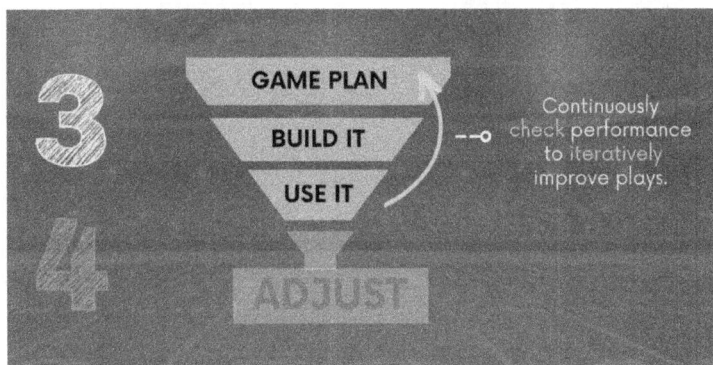

3

GAME PLAN

BUILD IT

USE IT

ADJUST

Continuously check performance to iteratively improve plays.

Ask yourself questions similar to those that coaches ask each week after watching film or practice to check how effectively you recently ran that play:

- What did you do well?
- What did you not do well?
- What are your best plays to run, and how can you align those to other scenarios?
- What are your weakest plays, and how can you keep practicing them or approach them differently?

Visualize the scenario, and imagine yourself making those incremental improvements from what you learned.

Your delivery or execution of these plays may not be perfect immediately, but over time these habits will help you practice your development plays more. As your professional season continues, you will become more natural and more effective. Think about a team's ability to run plays in the first few weeks of a season versus their ability to run the same plays later in the season. The difference is like night and day as the season goes on. In the worst-case scenario, if the plays are not working for you, then you confidently know they are not the right plays for you, and you remove them from your Play Sheet.

In the next chapter we will discuss how to use your Play Sheet over longer periods of time, how to reflect on how it is working, and how to make adjustments.

More Coaching Tips for Using Your Play Sheet

- **Play out mock scenarios**. You can also practice some of your concepts with friends, mentors, and peers or in smaller settings before you deploy them in your most crucial professional situations.

- **Seek 360-degree feedback**. Ask others to observe you running these plays. Let a mentor, a peer, or even a boss know what you are working on ahead of time, and ask them for candid feedback on how well you executed the play at certain moments. Collect their feedback as quickly as possible, and use it to help you reflect on how you performed that play and where to build off it. For example, one person on my team who used the Play Sheet years ago asked me to watch him while he gave a presentation at a town hall. He was a dynamic speaker, and his passion for the topic was evident, but his excitement often led him to speak too quickly for the audience to absorb the content of the message. As a result, he was working on his pace in presentations and had a play on his Play Sheet called "pause and breathe." Prior to taking the stage, he asked me to observe him and give him feedback after the presentation. Out of the gate he was a little fast, but at one point he glanced down to his speaker note card, and from that moment forward he was a new presenter. Later that afternoon, he called me and asked how he'd done. I gave him some positive feedback and some observations for improvement. I mentioned that he'd been much better after the point when I saw him glance at his notes, and he immediately responded, "I had my presentation plays on there, not my speaking points." I came to find out that he had several people planted in the audience that day to help observe his presentation skill development. We suggest you find others to help you as you work through the cognitive and associative phases of your skill development.

THIRD-QUARTER HIGHLIGHTS

In this chapter you accomplished a lot! You developed an intentional game plan for the next one to three months of your professional development. You built your Play Sheet. You started using your Play Sheet, and you started to evaluate how effective you were at running the plays on your Play Sheet.

- A popular iterative design method for continuous improvement is PDCA. Most coaches follow this process unknowingly, and this framework can help you in your continuous professional development.
  - Plan: Establish objectives and routines to deliver required results.
  - Do: Carry out the objectives.

- Check: Evaluate the results in terms of performance.
- Act (or Adjust): Maintain the change or begin the cycle again to further improve.

- **Plan: Build your game plan**. Like a football coach does early each week, you developed an intentional game plan for your development. You decided on areas of focus based on the situations at hand over the next month or quarter. This is your filter from Play Book to Play Sheet.

- **Plan: Build your Play Sheet**. You created your first Play Sheet. A Play Sheet in football is a list of plays used by the coach to call plays from. You added three to five categories of plays with three to five plays per category. Each play has a few succinct phrases to jog your memory so you can execute the concept of that play when needed. As you get more proficient and comfortable with this exercise, you can expand the scope of your Play Sheet and add more.

- You also added a key stat or reminder section to your Play Sheet and made your Play Sheet permanent by laminating and/or digitizing it.

- **Do: Begin using your Play Sheet**. To help yourself practice using your Play Sheet, you created a new pregame routine to plan for the day or week ahead. You also practiced using it in real-time scenarios to improve your ability to recall information in high-pressure situations.

- **Check: Evaluate your performance**. You started to carve out time to check the effectiveness of your plays and think about how you can iteratively improve them over this development cycle.

- You learned that the continued use of the Play Sheet and these routines will help you move these skills from the cognitive phase to the associative phase and finally to the autonomous phase. The autonomous phase is reached when we turn on autopilot, move the skill to the back of our proverbial mental filing cabinet, and stop paying conscious attention to it.

- You successfully started to mitigate the remaining sources of cognitive load.

- You learned a few other helpful strategies:
    - Outsmart yourself by setting reminders.
    - Minimize your risk by practicing in safe nonwork environments.

- Don't get discouraged if it does not work perfectly the first time, or even after multiple times.
- Seek frequent feedback from others to monitor your skill progression and development.

THE SEASON NEVER ENDS

MAKING ADJUSTMENTS

"Everyone wants
to be a success.
Not everyone is willing
to do what they have
to do to achieve it."

—NICK SABAN

FILM STUDY

EVERYONE LOVES A COMEBACK:
COACH DAVID DEAN'S ADJUSTMENTS LEAD TO VICTORY

Years ago at Valdosta State University, Offensive Coordinator David Dean and the Valdosta State Blazers were on the road at the University of Arkansas at Monticello. The higher-ranked Blazers were not as pumped for this game as they were for some bigger games later in the schedule. To start the game, the team went out and was flat. They were not executing, not doing the little things they needed to do, and not protecting the ball. Overall, they should have been playing much better.

At halftime Valdosta State trailed 3-0, and Coach Dean huddled his offensive staff first. He felt that his team was pressing and, as a result, making more mistakes. He and his staff drew up a script of five to seven plays to start the half that they hoped would give them some momentum, build their confidence, and allow them to start moving the chains.

Then he huddled his team and pulled out the old coach's motivational speech. He told his players, "Look, we are only down three points because our defense is playing great. If we go out there, focus on doing what we practiced, and just execute one play at a time, we will turn it around." He let the team know they would be making some adjustments; he had a set of plays from their Play Sheet that they were going to script to start the half. Coach Dean then simply said, "Let's go get 'em, boys," and the staff and players headed out of the locker room refocused, reenergized, and excited to turn the game around.

The Valdosta State offense received the ball to start the half. They quickly secured some first downs and then went on to score a touchdown on the opening series of the second half. Their confidence was restored, and the Blazers rode that adjustment and newly found confidence to a resounding 38–10 win, scoring all thirty-eight points in the second half.

MAKING ADJUSTMENTS

In the last chapter, I introduced the concept of continuous improvement. As you get comfortable using your Play Sheet and running plays daily, you will check or evaluate your performance running each play, and as time progresses, you will improve your performance running the play. These are tactical adjustments to enhance your execution of each play, but when and how should you take action to make more significant adjustments to your Play Sheet overall?

The last phase of the PDCA quality cycle is Act or Adjust. According to the American Society for Quality (ASQ), in this step you "take action based on what you learned in the study step. If the change did not work, go through the cycle again with a different plan. If you were successful, incorporate what you learned from the test into wider changes. Use what you learned to plan new improvements, beginning the cycle again."[16]

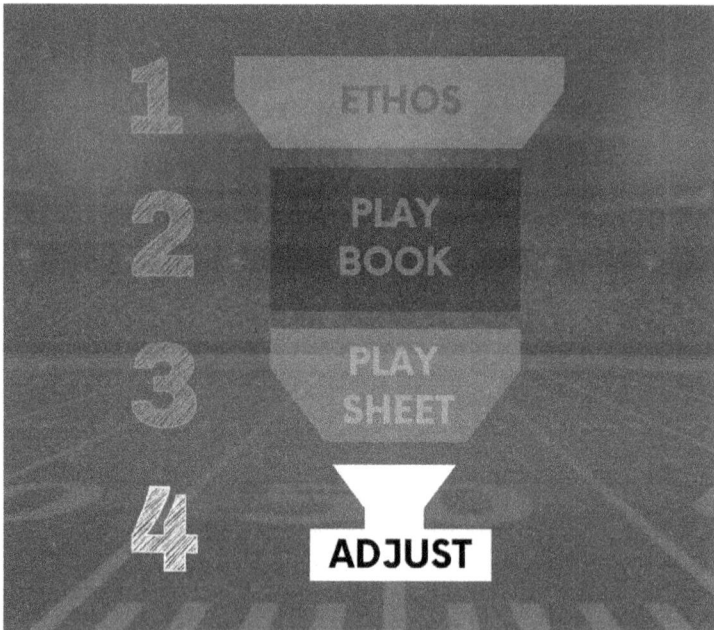

In this chapter we will discuss how to make long-term adjustments to your Play Sheet based on the success you have had running your plays from the previous time period and based on external factors that may require you to reevaluate the areas of focus on your Play Sheet. We will also look at

---

16 "What Is the Plan-Do-Check-Act (PDCA) Cycle?," American Society for Quality, accessed February 13, 2024, https://asq.org/quality-resources/pdca-cycle.

how to establish repeatable routines to do this in a cadence that suits you.

This section will be informative as you read it today, but it will be most helpful in the future. I recommend flagging this section because the practice of making adjustments to your objectives, your Play Book, or your Play Sheet will be constant if you hope to continue to grow not just today but throughout your career.

COACHING TIPS ON MAKING ADJUSTMENTS

Before we discuss how and when to make adjustments, here are some general coaching tips on making adjustments.

Adjusting Your Ethos May Be Warranted over Time

In Step 1, you created your ethos statement, and I stated that it should be long-lasting; your ethos statement should not be fluid and constantly changing. This is absolutely true, but over longer periods of time, things may change enough to warrant reevaluating and updating your ethos statement.

For example, in August of 2022, I had the honor of talking with Coach Sonny Dykes of Texas Christian University (TCU). Coach Dykes coached at Southern Methodist University the previous season, and as he moved from one program to the other, he had to evaluate the culture of his new school versus the culture of his previous one. As a result, he established a new culture, brand, and ethos for the Horned Frogs, who had finished 5–7 in 2021 under the previous coaching staff. He quickly built a fresh atmosphere and culture for TCU. He built his staff to further emulate the culture across the team and campus, and soon top-rated high school recruits and strong transfers from the transfer portal started to sign with TCU. Prior to the season, the Frogs had been projected to finish seventh in their own conference.

If you watched college football in 2022, you know that Coach Dykes and TCU shocked the college football world and went 9–0 in the Big 12 Conference and secured a trip to the College Football Playoff. In the semifinals, TCU upset the heavily favored University of Michigan and played the Georgia Bulldogs in the National Championship game. For decades, Coach Dykes had successfully coached at several top programs across the country, but when he moved to a new university, he had to adapt his ethos to align to the culture, values, and atmosphere of his new program. In your life and career, you may need to do the same when there are material changes to your environment. When material changes in your life or profession occur, it may behoove you to reassess your ethos statement—but remember that your ethos statement should very rarely change.

Avoid Change Saturation

Too many updates can create too much complexity, and sometimes simpler is better. We discussed the concept of cognitive load earlier; if you saturate yourself with too much change and too much information, you will never master the plays you are putting on your Play Sheet.

Don't Be Too Quick to Change Your Plays
Because They Worked a Few Times

Remember that the objective is to turn these plays into repeatable habits so they will withstand the test of time and won't quickly be forgotten.

Celebrate the plays that worked, and continue to run them. Most coaches will tell you they coach harder after a victory than a loss. It is easy for the team to get overconfident or complacent. Just because the play worked does not mean you can't run it better or master it further. There is a difference between good and great.

Don't Be Quick to Remove Plays Because They Didn't Work—
Doing So Could Be Premature

Sometimes you need to run the play a few times before the team executes it as designed. Be patient before you give up on a play you worked so hard on adding to your Play Sheet.

Sometimes coaches and teams struggle early and start to make adjustments too early rather than sticking to their game plan. Trust the process, trust the preparation, and trust the team before you jump to making too many changes. Sometimes the changes can even make things worse because you could introduce new information that causes more confusion and generates an even worse performance. Many high school coaches know that they can overcomplicate things and cause confusion if they are not careful.

Some Plays Could Be Your Key Plays for Life and Should Never Come Off

During a game, some coaches find a play on their Play Sheet that works big early, and they continue to run that play until the opponent can find a solution. If it ain't broke, don't fix it.

These plays can be confidence and momentum boosters. Most coaches script their key plays to start the game to move the chains early and build confidence in the players and then leverage those plays when they need a momentum shifter—a much-needed stop on defense or a first down on offense.

Use your Play Sheet the same way. Keep these tried-and-true plays to get the meeting off to a good start and build positive momentum when needed.

Keep Version Copies of Your Old Play Sheets

Sometimes what is old is new. Different stages of life may require you to run plays from your past, so to keep things organized, always keep previous versions of your Play Sheet on file. Think about a team playing the same opponent year after year. They can reference last year's version if not too many variables changed year over year. Business professionals sometimes have cyclical or annual events that could warrant using a particular Play Sheet again.

WHEN TO MAKE ADJUSTMENTS TO YOUR PLAY SHEET

People frequently ask me when is the right time to make changes or adjustments to their Play Sheet. There is no perfect answer to this, but adjustments and changes to your Play Sheet are necessary and inevitable.

There are two general instances in which you will update your Play Sheet. The first is on a predetermined, set cadence, and the second is situational.

Despite there being two instances when adjustments may be needed, it is imperative that you carve out time to evaluate the makeup of your Play Sheet on a consistent cadence that works for you. This needs to become a repeatable routine that occurs on a periodic basis. Those who intentionally dedicate time to make adjustments will figure out that a cadence that works for them will have a greater likelihood of maximizing their potential instead of just achieving one professional win.

Also, when updating your Play Sheet, focus on incremental versus iterative changes. In agile delivery terms, an increment is usually eight to twelve weeks, and an iteration (also called a sprint) is usually two weeks. Think increment rather than iteration as you perform this next step. As the season progresses, coaches continue to evaluate film and ask questions similar to those they ask after each game, but with a more sea-son-oriented mindset. In the last chapter, I discussed PDCA and the importance of carving out time to frequently check how well you performed your plays in the moment. If they were successful, then determine how to keep up the momentum and deploy them on a wider scale. If they are not crisp or need improvement, then evaluate how to run those plays better next time. These are iterative improvements. The act of adding or removing plays or categories of plays from your Play Sheet is more incremental in nature.

Another popular question is "As unexpected situations arise, can I make incremental changes to my Play Sheet at any time?"

When it comes to making holistic changes to the categories or plays on your Play Sheet, it is reasonable to make timely and off-cycle changes, but this should not be a frequent occurrence. If this behavior becomes persistent, then you may want to consider spending more time in Steps 7 and 8, building your game plan and your Play Sheet. Too many off-cycle edits may lead to an over complication of the process, a lack of focus and an inability to make skills natural and autonomous. This can cause a distraction and prevent you from achieving previously set objectives and key results.

An alternative to making Play Sheet changes off cadence is to move your latest ideas or plays to a parking lot in your Play Book. Flag them in your Play Book so when you reach the next cadence of updates, you can consider whether to prioritize them to your Play Sheet. If the play is new and completely aligned to your current set of plays, your objectives, and the key results associated with those objectives, then once again it is reasonable to add it to your Play Sheet. Sometimes, however, it is better to finish mastering what you started than to add more to your plate.

What I heard from most coaches, especially high school coaches who have less-experienced players, is that if they had to make major midgame adjustments, either something was really going wrong with their game plan or they were not executing their game plan well. Most of them mentioned that when they made adjustments, they tweaked what they had prepared all week rather than introducing major updates. They saw vulnerabilities in their team or strengths in their opponent that warranted attention, but at this point, many argued, trusting their process often was more effective than making wholesale changes in the middle of a game. If coaches are making major changes during the game, then they need to reevaluate how they prepared for that week. Simply put, the root cause of the problem was bad game planning or poor execution of the game plan in the game.

The moral of the story here is that minimal (off-cycle) adjustments should be needed between your set cadences if you are making enough time to review your performance in the previous cycle and make the necessary adjustments to your Play Sheet during the time you set on a monthly or quarterly basis.

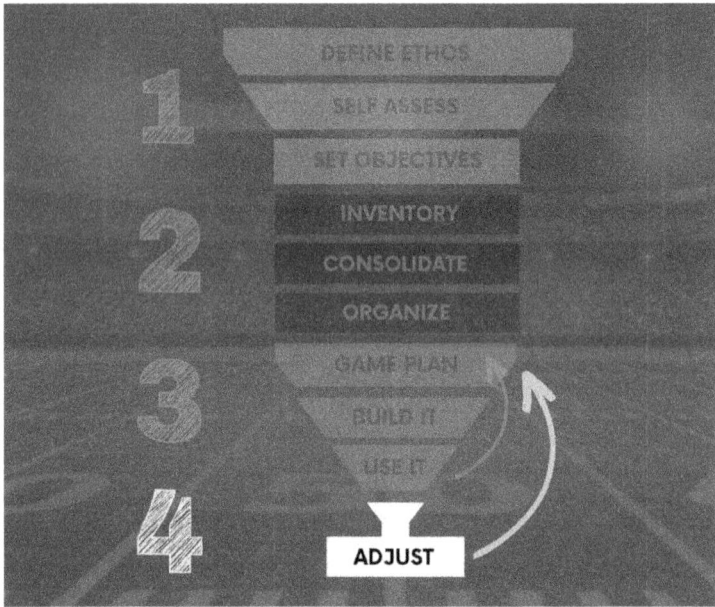

Adjust: Establish repeatable routines to perform retrospectives to adjust your game plan and Play Sheet over time. Master a category of plays and choose new focus areas or adjust categories based on situational changes.

FILM STUDY

Adjustments Led to a High School Playoff Number-One Seed: Coach David Branscom

Fall Friday nights in South Texas are everything you have heard and read about. High school rivalries are as big here as they are in some college conferences. In 2018, this was definitely true in 6A Region IV District 28 (the San Antonio, Texas, area). Three schools were vying for the top seed heading into the playoffs. Earlier in the year, the Warren Warriors had gone on the road and upset the Brennan Bears 33–21. Then a few weeks later, the Brennan Bears went on the road and beat the Brandeis Broncos 27–20. Several weeks into the season, it looked like these three teams would be the contenders for the top seed in their division.

The Brandeis Broncos and Head Coach David Branscom needed to beat the Warren Warriors in week eight, win out after that, and try to create the largest point differential among the three teams that could all end up with one loss at the end of the regular season.

Against Brennan in week six, they ran their core defensive formation and play set, but Brennan's coaching staff must have found a vulnerability in the Brandeis defense during their Friday-to-Friday process. Early in the second quarter, as Coach Brennan recalls vividly, the team was exposed, and Brennan threw a seventy-two-yard touchdown pass. Later in the game, they had another long pass that set up a short touchdown run, and with less than a minute to go, Brennan once again attacked the weakness they'd identified in Brandeis's defense and threw a game-winning forty-two-yard touchdown pass.

Coach Branscom immediately asked himself and his staff the same questions I asked you earlier: "What did we not do well? What are our gaps, and how do we start to close this gap in our game plan and our approach to coaching the team going forward?"

He realized they needed to adjust their scheme and formation coverages on defense to prevent the big plays they'd allowed against Brennan. This required Branscom to dig into his Play Book and required his defensive coaching staff to coach up the team on the new approach and work to implement it immediately. This was a risk, but he felt it was less than the risk of Warren and other teams later in the year seeing what had occurred on the Brennan film and adding it to their call scripts.

In week seven, they got to try it out and shake off some rust in a home matchup against Holmes High School, and it worked. Holmes was shocked by the change in scheme.

One week later, the Brandeis Broncos traveled to the Warren Warriors for a critical matchup that would determine the division winner. Coach Branscom and his Brandeis Broncos confused Warren with this new scheme and formation and pulled off a big road win, 41–19, which put the Broncos in a three-way tie for the division lead. They also now had the point differential tiebreaker with this twenty-two-point victory.

Coach Branscom and the Brandeis Broncos ran the table the rest of the regular season and clinched the number-one seed in the division. This allowed them to avoid the top-ranked West Lake Chaparrals until at least the fourth round of the playoffs rather than facing them in the second round if they had not won the division. Brandeis won their first three play-off games but unfortunately lost their fourth-round matchup to West Lake.

According to Coach Branscom, not only did this midseason adjustment lead to a more successful 2018 season, but the momentum and playoff experience also bled into the 2019 season, when they went 9–0 in the district and 13–1 overall.

Every week, coaches like Coach Branscom reflect on what their team and players are doing well and not so well. As the coaching staff identifies these strengths or potential gaps, they start to problem-solve what that means to their approach going forward.

What Should Your Repeatable Cadence Look Like?

The Agile Manifesto emphasizes the importance of continuous improvement through the following principle: "At regular intervals, the team reflects on how to become more effective, then tunes and adjusts its behavior accordingly."[17] One form of agile is SAFe, which stands for Scaled Agile Framework. It is generally used to implement agile principles in large organizations. In the Scaled Agile Framework, there are several concepts that are analogous to the week-over-week repeatable processes used by coaches. While opportunities to improve can and should occur continuously throughout, applying

---

17   Beck et. al., "Principles Behind the Agile Manifesto."

some structure, cadence, and synchronization helps to ensure that there is also time set aside to identify improvements across multiple areas more holistically.

The creation of your OKRs, Play Book, and Play Sheet is not a one-and-done exercise. As new information is learned, skills are mastered, and external factors change, these items may need to evolve. The key is to create a periodic cadence to dedicate time to inspect and adapt accordingly. Find a cadence that works for you, and review what went well and what did not go so well. You will not have game film to review at the end of each week, but the process to make changes or incremental improvements draws parallels. You may not do this every Sunday, but the approach to inspect or review the past to make adjustments and adapt for tomorrow is remarkably similar to the coaches' process. I recommend reviewing at least sixty to ninety days of performance to effectively evaluate your improvement across categories of plays and plays within categories.

To create a baseline, block off a couple of hours ninety days from the day you start using your Play Sheet, and schedule that as a recurring meeting on your calendar. This may not be the perfect cadence for you, but the important point is that you set time to perform this exercise on a consistent basis. You will get better with each increment of time.

When you do determine the appropriate cadence, you should dedicate several hours to perform a ceremony called an inspect and adapt to conduct a review and adjust what categories and plays should stay, be updated, be removed, or be added to your Play Sheet.

In professional settings, an inspect and adapt ceremony is usually held at the end of each quarter. There are two major parts to this event, just as the name suggests.

- Part 1: A team demonstrates the work delivered or completed in the previous quarter (inspect).

- Part 2: Via a structured problem-solving workshop, teams perform a retrospective to reflect and determine areas of improvement to be added to their backlog of work (adapt).

I have participated in and hosted many of these sessions throughout my career. At one company, we carved out an entire day to host each of our inspect and adapt sessions. They included business leaders, technology leaders, project teams, change and communication managers, portfolio and project managers, and more. It was always hard to make time, but when the group dedicated the time to do this event, the engagement, team building, learning, and incremental improvements were remarkable. They also included tons of coffee and food, and it was always nice to get the teams together in person to build our team dynamic.

The day was split into two parts. During the first half of the day, all the teams reviewed their initial objectives for that increment, described the work they had completed and the value it created, and then showed a visual demonstration of the work completed over the last ninety days.

The second half of the day focused on the adapt, or adjust, exercise. Teams broke up into groups and reflected on how well their work aligned to the objectives and discussed the top issues or impediments they faced in order to complete the work. Then groups performed a problem-solving exercise to prioritize the top things to improve over the next increment and laid out solutions to do so.

STEP 10: CREATE YOUR OWN REPEATABLE ROUTINE TO MAKE ADJUSTMENTS

On the day and time you block off in your calendar, you will perform your own inspect and adapt session. Here is a proposed agenda for that session. Please note that over time you will get a feel for how often you want to conduct this exercise (monthly, quarterly, semiannually, etc.). The key is to be consistent in your cadence.

Inspect

- Reflect on all the accomplishments you made over this period of time. Put them into words, and store them in your preferred medium. Celebrate your wins.

- Bring out your ethos statement, OKRs, and game plan. How much measurable progress did you make against them over this time? Ask yourself what went well and what needs improvement, and document these as well.

- Review the holistic progress you made on your categories of plays. For example, if you had five plays on time management, how much did you improve on the overall category of time management? Earlier in the book, you performed a gap analysis on certain skills. Did each skill advance from a five to a seven? Have you mastered each skill, or do you need to continue to work on a skill over the next development increment?

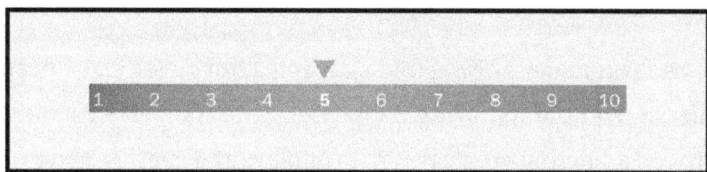

- Assess which plays in that category are working well and which plays need more practice. Over time, if a play does not feel right or work for you, that is okay as well. Not every play is made for every team, and not every idea or concept is made for you or your style. Remove the play from your Play Sheet. Keep it in your

Play Book, though, because although it may not work at this season of your professional career, it may work in the future.

- It is also helpful to look at your upcoming calendar of events or key milestones ahead and determine whether changes should be made due to what is most important for the next increment of time.

Adapt/Adjust

To adjust and adapt over time, repeat Steps 7 and 8 from the previous chapter based on the retrospective you performed here.

- Build your game plan for the next increment of time.
- Build your Play Sheet for the next increment of time.

As you make a new game plan and adjust your Play Sheet, please read the following subsections that provide coaching tips on adjusting your categories of plays and specific plays in your categories.

Suggestions on Adjusting Your Categories of Plays

Earlier in the book, several coaches talked about how once they saw what the opponent was good at, they immediately eliminated a portion of their Play Book and narrowed down their plays to only certain categories for that opponent.

THE SEASON NEVER ENDS

Here are some possible indications that you may want to change out an entire category of plays from your Play Sheet. (For example, you may remove presentation plays and add in time management plays.)

Role Changes Due to Promotion, Organizational Changes, a New Boss, New Direct Reports, or Movement to a New Company. In football a different opponent may require you to play to different strengths, so you must adapt to win this game despite your success in previous games. Also, sometimes an injury to one of your or your opponent's key players may change the dynamic enough that it warrants adjustments to the game plan and plays.

Any impactful change to your team or your work environment may warrant you focusing on skills other than those you'd planned to focus on. This could trigger the need for you to prioritize one skill category over another due to recent changes in your ecosystem.

A few years ago, I was impacted by a company reorganization, moved into a new department, and had a new boss overnight. My approach and style to meet his expectations needed to shift, so I immediately added a set of communication plays that would help me be more effective with him. These had always been in my Play Book but were not on my Play Sheet at the time. This change in leader required me to prioritize this category of plays over another.

Introduction of a New Category That You Were Not Previously Aware Of. Since you are reading this book, I assume you are a continuous learner. You will undoubtedly come across new concepts, approaches, and ideas that were not on your radar when you last built your Play Sheet. A few years ago, I read *10% Happier* by Dan Harris, and the book convinced me to start meditating. I was hooked and still am to this day. A few weeks after reading that book, the positive impacts I was seeing from meditation and the principles I was learning led me to add an entire category of plays called meditation and mindfulness to my Play Book and Play Sheet.

Proficiency in Certain Skills—Habits Have Been Formed. You have arrived at the "autonomous stage" or are running these plays on autopilot, so it is a sensible time to clear some space to build proficiency in other areas. You can keep these in your Play Book, but they may have run their course in your Play Sheet.

Milestones or Changes in Your Mission. New Year's resolutions, marriages, divorces, having kids, and major life changes sometimes make you reevaluate your goals and priorities. As this occurs, it may drive the need to adjust the categories of plays on your Play Sheet.

When I became a new dad, time management became more important than ever. I did not want to miss time with my wife and kids, so I needed to prioritize time management plays on my Play Sheet to improve work-life balance and be the father and husband they deserved.

Suggestions on Adjusting Certain Plays from a Category of Plays

Here are some triggers that may cause you to consider changing out specific plays in some of your play categories. (For example, you may remove certain leadership plays from your general leadership category.)

The Individual Play Has Become an Autonomous Skill or Habit

This contradicts some advice in the previous section, but you can't keep every concept or play on your Play Sheet forever. It's great to have plays on there as a reminder to play to your strengths, but you may not need any reminders of some plays.

For example, a mentee of mine had "slow down to speed up" as a play under their time management category. I knew that this person blocked off 6:30 a.m. to 7:00 a.m. every day to slow down and prepare. They still had that play on their Play Sheet, yet this play had been part of their daily routine for years and was definitely an ingrained habit. This person could start adding new plays to expand their breadth of plays under time management.

Play Does Not Match Your Style

Sometimes you learn about a concept or get advice that works for others, but it just doesn't feel natural or simply it may just not work for you. That's okay. Don't give up on plays immediately, but at a certain point, you may just know that this concept is not suited for you. Don't force it, and once you reach that point, clear some space for other plays in that category.

You Found Better Plays in a Certain Category

I have found that as people really start researching certain topics, they find a lot of concepts or information to improve in that category. You may have seven plays in a category, and as you learn more about that subject matter, you might find plays that suit you better or that you feel should be prioritized over other plays. This is like prioritizing your backlog. Sometimes it's okay to put some things below the line to move other things above the line.

Recall that Coach Lincoln Riley has a cut line of twenty-eight plays for his Play Sheet. The twenty-ninth play might be a good play, but he forces himself to find the twenty-eight best plays for each game. This process is all about maximizing your potential, so sometimes certain plays just need to take a back seat to make room for those that will make you more successful at this moment in time.

In this chapter, you were provided several suggestions on when and how to make adjustments to your ethos statement,

THE SEASON NEVER ENDS

Play Book, game plan, and Play Sheet. Depending on how well you are improving and what is needed going forward, this step could be a time for you to slow down, reflect, and take action on where to focus and what to do next. It is imperative that this becomes a simple, repeatable process for your development. You may not see your results every month or quarter, but if you are willing to stay committed, you will start to see incremental strides in your development.

FOURTH-QUARTER HIGHLIGHTS

- According to the American Society for Quality (ASQ), the A in the PDCA cycle is Act or Adjust. In this step, you "take action based on what you learned in the study step. If the change did not work, go through the cycle again with a different plan. If you were successful, incorporate what you learned from the test into wider changes. Use what you learned to plan new improvements, beginning the cycle again."

- Be aware of these tips when adjusting your Play Sheet:
  - Changing plays too often may lead to change saturation and an inability to improve the skill and achieve your objectives and key results.

- Don't be too quick to change your plays because they worked a few times.
- Don't be quick to remove plays because they didn't work; you could be doing so prematurely.
- Some plays could be your key plays for life and should never come off.

- This is not a one-and-done process. It requires continuous relentless improvement. Your development never stops and requires you to establish a repeatable cadence to make adjustments. The Agile Manifesto emphasizes the importance of continuous improvement through the following principle: "At regular intervals, the team reflects on how to become more effective, then tunes and adjusts its behavior accordingly." Find a cadence that works for you to perform your own inspect and adapt session, but I recommend monthly or quarterly. Those who establish this repeatable routine have a greater likelihood of maximizing their potential.

- Over time, focus on incremental improvements to your Play Sheet rather than iterative enhancements to the plays on them.

- Sometimes situational events may warrant immediate updates to your game plan or Play Sheet, but this should not be a frequent occurrence. Examples of events that can trigger the need for updates include organizational changes, major life events, change in job or company, and economic swings.

- When making adjustments, you should consider whether you will change entire categories of plays, change certain plays within a category, or add more plays due to new sources of information.

In summary, you can now establish personalized repeatable routines to make periodic adjustments to your tools and make incremental impacts to your development.

WILL YOU BE A ONE AND DONE OR A HALL OF FAMER?

"Let me tell you what winning means...you're willing to go longer, work harder, give more than anyone else."

—VINCE LOMBARDI

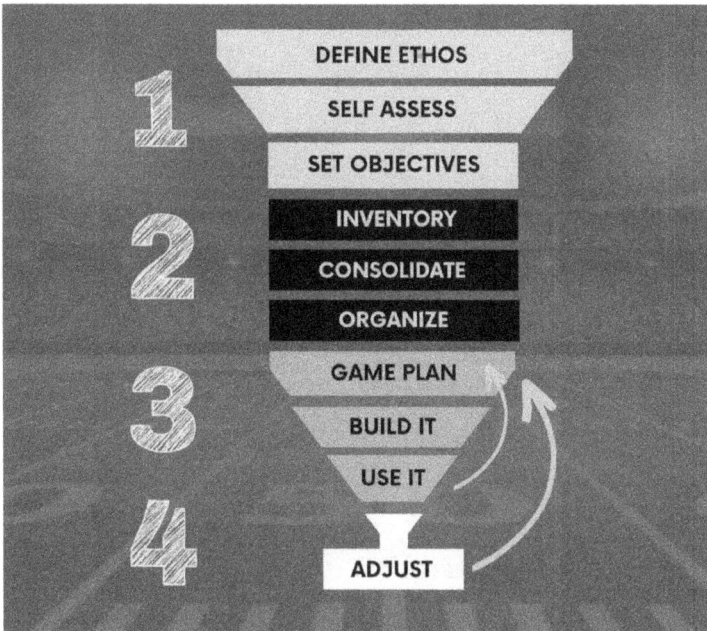

Over four quarters of this book, I've coached you through ten steps that can help you achieve more professional wins. The first quarter focused on you taking a look inward and outward to determine your ethos, your style, and the areas you want to focus on developing. In the second quarter, you inventoried, consolidated, and organized all your development content into a single source, your Play Book. Then in the third quarter, you narrowed your focus to the next three to six months and developed a game plan and a Play Sheet to help you iteratively improve certain professional skills and areas of development. Finally, in the fourth quarter, you learned how to establish repeatable routines to enable you to evaluate your performance over time, adjust your approach based on recent learnings, and hopefully master certain areas of your career.

Now take a moment to step back and look at those steps collectively. When added together, they form an image of a trophy. This may be a cliché, but once you complete all these steps, you deserve to be rewarded, and as a result, you have earned a trophy for your hard work, dedication, failures, and successes. Winning once does not mean you will become a long-term success or guarantee you will accomplish all your long-term aspirations; therefore, you need to continue this process in perpetuity. Ask yourself: will you have one winning season or will you create a culture of ongoing success?

FILM STUDY

THE SEASON MAY END,
BUT THE HARD WORK CONTINUES

In 2021, then-sixty-nine-year-old Nick Saban won his seventh
NCAA football championship. What is amazing about this leg-
endary coach is that he never stops moving forward, no matter how many wins he captures. His continuous improvement
is showcased every time he wins a national title, and 2021 was
no different.

Despite going 13-0 and winning 52-24, Saban was interviewed multiple times after the game and the following day,
and his responses demonstrate why he has won seven championships while many feel lucky to have won one.

In his Tuesday morning press conference, Saban said, "The to-do list started after the game last night."

In that same press conference, he explained, "It's an ongoing process, building a team. I don't think you can fall asleep at the switch for a minute if you want to try to do it the right way for your players and your program."

Do you aspire to be a Hall of Famer in your industry or company, like Nick Saban, or do you want to be a one-win success story? The most successful coaches are always looking forward. They never stop improving, recruiting, prepping, coaching, or developing. The longer you develop and improve your system, the more professional wins you will achieve.

Now let me add the caveat that not everyone is the best of the best like Saban. Lord knows I am nowhere close, but the point of the story is to never stop improving, adapting, learning, and progressing. The process for coaches never stops. There are always new players, new challenges, new opponents, new teams, and new rules to the game. The same holds true in the professional arena, where businesspeople face organizational changes, new leaders, new markets, new jobs, and new life situations.

So how high you climb or how much success you achieve will depend on your ability to practice relentless continuous improvement.

I hope this process is simple and repeatable enough for you to finally apply what you learned in those critical professional situations. I also hope you celebrate those wins with those who helped you get there: your team, your family, and anyone else who played a role in your success.

But don't get too complacent, comfortable, or confident if you want to see ongoing success. My hope is that you never stop adding to your Play Book or updating your Play Sheet as you progress and work to leave a lasting legacy in your career.

COACHING TIPS ON USING THIS SYSTEM OVER TIME

Here are a few coaching tips to use over time:

- **Always keep your mission and ethos front and center**. Let it guide you and remind you of your desired destination.

- **Constantly assess your skill maturity**. Over time you will master certain skills, or certain skills will arise that are needed to remain relevant. These ongoing self-assessments will help guide you on what categories are important to your Play Book and Play Sheet.

- **Keep updating your OKRs**. Your objectives should always be aspirational. If they become easy to accomplish as you mature in your domain, you need to elevate the challenge to yourself.

- **Keep your inventory updated**. A common mistake is to build your Play Book and never look back at it in its entirety. Some plays from long ago may be more relevant than ever; therefore, the more organized your Play Book is, the more easily you will be able to access information from it when necessary.

- **Keep your Play Book consolidated and organized**. Like a digital folder, a bookshelf, or a closet, the amount of stuff in your Play Book will grow over time. Keep it in one place, and spend time keeping it organized so locating ideas or concepts will remain easy for you when it is time to build your future game plans and Play Sheets. This will always help mitigate cognitive load.

- **Share it**. The more you share this process and the development plays within it, the more you will see people benefiting from it, and over time they will start to share their best practices and development plays with you. This is the multiplier effect. When I started sharing my Play Sheet with people years ago, those people would always send me a copy of their Play Sheet. Often when looking at their Play Sheet, I would find an interesting concept and simply ask that person about it. This expanded my knowledge set and led to some great practices that I would have never otherwise discovered.

- **Scale it**. Once you start to mature in your professional life, it may be time for you to apply this framework to other aspects of your life. I created other Play Sheets that helped me tremendously. I created an interview Play Sheet and a parenting Play Sheet. As the father of two young children, I have consumed countless sources of parenting help. In my house, my wife and I have laminated sheets of paper with plays around routines, sibling rivalries, the use of consequences versus encouragement, and other parenting tips we have learned or heard along the way. Also, anytime I interview for a new job, I have a Play Sheet of all my accomplishments, skills, answers to interview questions, and more to help me quickly recall my experience and to answer any zinger the interviewer throws my way.

As you finish reading this book, I would love for you to consider doing two things:

- Take time to reflect on the teacher, coach, boss, or mentor who helped you to get where you are today. Literally call them and sincerely thank them for their investment in you.

- Please share this book with someone you think could benefit from it: a student, mentee, or employee on your team or in your area. If you talk to any coach, they will tell you that the most fulfilling part of the job is seeing the development, growth, and success of their players and staff. Years of seeing their hard work and determination firsthand overshadows any loss they may encounter during a season. The legacy of a high school or college football coach is the number of young men they mold into high-performing adults who excel in whatever path they take in life. In an interview, the great Tony Dungy once said, "It's about the journey—mine and yours—and the lives we touch, the legacy we can leave, and the world we can change for the better." Over the years, I have personally benefited from this process, and each professional win felt incredible, but none of those wins compared to the feeling I got when I started mentoring others on using the Play Sheet process and seeing their success.

It is my sincere hope that the learnings from this framework and the coaches you met help you achieve more professional wins, more career goals, and success in your life and your career. Thank you for putting in the time and the hard work and for reading my book. Now it's time for you to get out there and give it all you've got.

As they say in football huddles across the country, break on three.

Ready?

One, two, three, break!

ACKNOWLEDGMENTS

Authoring this book was a life goal for me, and I need to personally thank the team that helped make it happen.

- First, my amazing wife, Erica, for all her support and for pushing me to tackle this life goal
- The Scribe Guided Author community and the Scribe team
- The American Football Coaches Association (AFCA)
- The Texas High School Coaches Association (THSCA)
- The countless coaches and executives who spent time sharing their processes and experiences to develop the Play Sheet. Please see the following roster of coaches.

THE ROSTER OF COACHES

- Coach Tony Elliott
  - University of Virginia: Head coach, 2022–present
  - Clemson University: Offensive coordinator, 2015–2022
  - Two-time CFP National Championship winner
  - Two-time CFP National Championship runner-up
  - Clemson University: Running backs coach, 2011–2014
  - Furman University: Wide receivers coach, 2008–2010
  - South Carolina State University: Wide receivers coach, 2006–2007

- Coach Jake Spavital
  - Baylor University: Offensive coordinator and QB coach, 2024
  - University of California: Offensive coordinator and QB coach, 2023
  - Texas State University: Head coach, 2019–2022
  - West Virginia University: Offensive coordinator and QB coach, 2017–2018
  - University of California: Offensive coordinator and QB coach, 2016

- Texas A&M University: Offensive coordinator and QB coach, 2013–2015
- West Virginia University: QB coach, 2011–2012
- Graduate assistant under Gus Malzahn, Dana Holgorsen, and Mike Leach at schools including the University of Tulsa, the University of Houston, and Oklahoma State University.

- Coach Liam Klein
  - Kennesaw State University: Defensive line coach and recruiting coordinator, 2014–present
  - Georgia Institute of Technology (Georgia Tech): Director of player personnel, 2007–2014
  - Harvard University: Linebackers/safeties coach, 2002
  - Lafayette College: Defensive line coach, 2001

- Coach Dominic Anderson
  - 2022 Chicago Bears Bill Walsh Diversity Coaching Fellowship recipient
  - Fayetteville State University: Defensive coordinator/linebackers coach, 2021–present
  - University of Pikesville (Kentucky): Defensive coordinator, 2017–2021
  - South Plantation High School (Plantation, Florida): Head coach, 2016

- University of St. Francis (III) NAIA: Defensive backs coach, 2015
- Illinois State University: Defensive backs coach, 2011–2014
- Wake Forest University: Graduate assistant

- Coach David Dean
  - University of West Florida: Head coach, 2017–present
  - Georgia Southern University: OC/WR coach, 2016
  - Valdosta State University: Head coach, 2007–2015
  - Two-time DII National Championship winner (2007, 2012)
  - Valdosta State University: Offensive coordinator/quarterbacks coach, 2000–2005

- Coach Roger Harriott
  - St. Thomas Aquinas High School (Fort Lauderdale, Florida): Head coach, 2015–present
  - Florida High School State 7A Championship winner 2015, 2016, 2019, 2020 (National Championship winner 2020), 2021, 2022, 2023
  - Florida Atlantic University: Assistant coach/running backs coach, 2014

- University School of Nova Southeastern University: Head Coach, 2006–2013

- Coach David Branscom
  - Allen High School (Allen, Texas): Defensive coordinator, 2021–present
  - Louis D. Brandeis High School (San Antonio, Texas): Head coach, 2017–2021
  - Louis D. Brandeis High School (San Antonio, Texas): Defensive coordinator/linebackers coach, 2015–2017
  - University of Mary-Hardin Baylor: Assistant coach/special teams coordinator/linebackers coach, 2004–2015

- Coach Charles Bruce
  - Louis D. Brandeis High School (San Antonio, Texas): Head coach, 2021–present
  - Wagner High School (San Antonio, Texas): Head coach, 2013–2021
  - Coach Darrell Andrus
  - Jourdanton High School (San Antonio, Texas): Head coach, 2014–present
  - Flour Bluff High School (Corpus Christi, Texas): Head coach, 2005–2014

- Coach Sonny Dykes
  - Texas Christian University: Head coach, 2022–present
  - Southern Methodist University: Head coach, 2018–2021
  - Texas Christian University: Head coach/offensive analyst, 2017
  - University of California: Head coach, 2013–2016
  - Louisiana Tech University: Head coach, 2010–2012

- Coach Dana Dimel
  - University of Texas at El Paso: Head coach, 2018–2023
  - Kansas State University: Offensive coordinator, 2009–2017
  - University of Arizona: Tight end/running backs coach 2006–2008
  - University of Houston: Head coach, 2000–2002
  - University of Wyoming: Head coach, 1997–1999

- Coach Chris Castillo
  - Lehman High School (San Antonio, Texas): Head coach, 2023–present
  - Highlands High School (San Antonio, Texas): Head coach, 2020–2022

- Sunset High School (Dallas, Texas): Head coach, 2016–2019
- Johns Hopkins University: Defensive line coach, 2013–2014

- Coach Darrell Andrus
  - Jourdanton High School (Jourdanton, Texas): Head Coach 2014–present
  - Flour Bluff High School (Corpus Christi, Texas): Head Coach 2004–2014

- And many more who preferred to be anonymous in this book

FURTHER READING AND ADDITIONAL RESOURCES

- Scaled Agile, Inc.; *www.scaledagileframework.com*
- ASQ, American Society for Quality; *www.asq.org*
- Franklin Covey; *www.franklincovey.com*

Roetzel, Peter Gordon. "Information Overload in the Information Age: A Revwiew of the Literature from Business Administration, Business Psychology, and Related Disciplines with a Bibliometric Approach and Framework Development." *Business Research* 12 (2019): 479–522. https://doi.org/10.1007/s40685-018-0069-z.

binti Suhaimi, Farah Amirah and Norhayati binti Hussin. "The Influence of Information Overload on Students' Academic Performance." *International Journal of Academic Research in Business and Social Sciences* 7, no. 8 (2017): 760–766. http://dx.doi.org/10.6007/IJARBSS/v7-i8/3292.

Indeed Editorial Team. "How to Write a Personal Mission Statement (with Examples)." Indeed. Last modified October 22, 2022. https://ca.indeed.com/career-advice/career-development/personal-mission-statement.

Forbes Coaches Council. "13 Ways You Can Craft a Strong Personal Mission Statement." *Forbes*, November 7, 2017. https://www.forbes.com/sites/forbescoachescouncil/2017/11/07/13-ways-you-can-craft-a-strong-personal-mission-statement.

Battista, Judy. "Coaches Use Laminated Game Outlines for Any Situation." *New York Times*, October 27, 2006. https://www.nytimes.com/2006/10/27/sports/football/27coaches.html.

Simpson, Kenny. "How to Build a Call Sheet." YouTube video, 13:06, January 6, 2022. https://www.youtube.com/watch?v=YeKJmqQIlP4.

Kalb, Matt. "Cheat Sheets—Making the Most out of Your Play
    Calling System." *American Football Monthly*, February
    2014. https://www.americanfootballmonthly.com/
    Subaccess/articles.php?article_id=6185&output=article.

Johnson, Richard. "There's Tons of Other Stuff in
    Your Football Team's Playbook." Banner Society,
    August 15, 2019. https://www.bannersociety.
    com/2019/8/15/20726587/what-is-in-a-playbook-football.